PRAISE FOR
On Mindful Democracy

"*On Mindful Democracy* is a profoundly wise and timely offering—a call to awaken our hearts to the truth of our interdependence. With clarity and compassion, Jeremy Engels invites us to step out of division and into presence, to remember that democracy is not a battle but a shared practice of care. This book is a balm for weary spirits and a guiding light for those longing to heal our fractured world—from the inside out."

— TARA BRACH, author of *Radical Compassion: Learning to Love Yourself and Your World with the Practice of RAIN*

"Democracy is tested daily by forces of division, fear, and inequality. On Mindful Democracy reminds us that democracy is not merely a system of government but a daily practice of compassion, mindfulness, and interdependence. As a mayor and global advocate for compassion, I have seen how communities are transformed when people choose care over conflict and belonging enemyship. Jeremy David Engels offers a hopeful and practical path toward a democracy that heals and unites—a vision every leader should embrace."

— GREG FISCHER, former president of the US Conference of Mayors and mayor of Louisville, Kentucky 2011–2023

"Jeremy Engels invites us to reimagine our political system in his timely and refreshing take *On Mindful Democracy*, reminding us what a democracy can be when we recognize our interdependence and celebrate our differences."

— SHARON SALZBERG, author of *Lovingkindness: The Revolutionary Art of Happiness*

"Jeremy Engels writes with clarity and insight on the fruitful interdependence of mindfulness and democracy. This is certainly a topic of major interest to all of us concerned with our shared planetary future. His fresh spirit and authentic voice are not only refreshing but enlightening. Read this and be transformed!"

— MARY EVELYN TUCKER, cofounder of the Yale Forum on Religion and Ecology and coauthor of *Journey of the Universe*

"*On Mindful Democracy* is a book of practical wisdom. This timely book bridges the gap between pragmatism and idealism. We need to read this book and then to embrace and practice the principle of interdependence as Jeremy Engels describes it in politics as well as in our daily lives."

—SATISH KUMAR, editor emeritus of *Resurgence* magazine and author of *Radical Love*

"At a time of angry words and fragmented information, *On Mindful Democracy* offers a much-needed vision of wholeness. Engels combines the knowledge of a rhetoric scholar with the insight of a mindfulness teacher to uncover the true meaning of democracy—the word comes from the Greek roots for 'community' and 'power.' This is a handbook for true interdependence, a practical guide to staying open and curious while engaging with all sorts of people and ideas. As Engels notes of social media, 'When your body tightens and constricts, it's time to take a break.' Reading this book does the opposite—it leaves you feeling hopeful and spacious in both body and mind."

—JENNIE ROTHENBERG GRITZ, writer, *Smithsonian* magazine

"*On Mindful Democracy* reframes democracy not as a battle to be fought but as a practice of care, and not as a pathway to independence but a reminder of our interdependence. Jeremy David Engels offers a powerful vision of how mindfulness can help heal our fractured world."

—KAZU HAGA, author of *Fierce Vulnerability: Healing from Trauma, Emerging through Collapse*

"A deeply healing vision for how we might meet these fractured times with presence, open hearts, and the courage to build beloved community. Jeremy Engels reawakens the true spirit of democracy as a mindful practice of care, compassion, and interdependence."

—BANAFSHEH SAYYAD, author of *Dance of Oneness: Awaken, Heal, and Transform Through Embodied Love and Light*

"Fighting doesn't work. Jeremy Engels's Declaration of Interdependence reminds us that interbeing and interconnectedness are more than ideas—they are concrete practices that reconnect us with the world. His text invites us to move beyond black-and-white thinking and to look with eyes of loving-kindness at our so-called 'political enemies' and to understand them better."

—KAI ROMHARDT, chair of the Network for Mindful Business and author of *We Are the Economy: The Buddhist Way of Work, Consumption, and Money*

"Jeremy Engels provides an audacious, insightful, and long overdue reappraisal of what ails contemporary democracies. Encapsulated in his revised 'Declaration of Interdependence,' Engels draws on Eastern spiritual traditions to prescribe mindfulness and compassion as the best remedies for the ills of political polarization and demonization that are pushing democracies around the world to the abyss of populist authoritarianism and outright technofascism. Don't miss this important book!"

> —MANFRED B. STEGER, author of *Globalization: A Very Short Introduction*

"In *On Mindful Democracy*, Engels summons us to care for our democracy, now. From a place of deep practice and teaching, he has written a concise and cogent guide for practicing democracy in the midst of present-day despair. He challenges us to deeply consider the common ground of interdependence as an indisputable fact of life. Engels explores the salient question: How do we practice democracy? Yes, democracy is an everyday practice of life-affirming actions by you and me! This mighty little book should be on everyone's bedside table to be read daily for transforming our hearts and minds in service of our mutually shared lives."

> —WENDY EGYOKU NAKAO, abbot emeritus of the Zen Center of Los Angeles

"In person, Jeremy's calm and centered presence feels like a warm blanket of comfort and peace. Through his writing, he is somehow able to transport that essential quality to make the book be an anchor in a sea of uncertainty. Read this book—it will change your life. If enough of us embody the insights presented here, it might even change the world."

> —LARA HEIMANN, founder and CEO of LYT yoga

"Mindful insight can bring us to a place of peace, a place beyond the false bravado of strongly held opinions and attitudes. Such a transition must be made for democracy to become real. Power resides with the people in a functioning democracy. This book gives practical advice on how to recover human agency through gentle, ongoing awareness of our inter-dependence."

> —CHRISTOPHER KEY CHAPPLE, Doshi Professor of Indic and Comparative Theology and director of the master of arts in Yoga Studies program, Loyola Marymount University

ON MINDFUL
DEMOCRACY

ON MINDFUL DEMOCRACY

A Declaration of
INTERDEPENDENCE
to Mend a Fractured World

JEREMY DAVID ENGELS

BERKELEY, CALIFORNIA

Parallax Press
PO Box 7355
Berkeley, CA 94707
parallax.org

Parallax Press is the publishing division of
Plum Village Community of Engaged Buddhism, Inc.

Cover art and design by Katie Eberle
Interior design by Maureen Forys, Happenstance Type-O-Rama
Author photograph by Anna Sunderland Engels

Printed in the United States of America by Versa Press

Parallax Press's authorized representative in the EEA is
SARL Boutique La Bambouseraie Point UH, Le Pey, 24240 Thénac, France
Email: europe@parallax.org

Disclaimer: The advice in this book is intended for general information
purposes only. Any application of the material set forth in the following
pages is at the reader's discretion and is their sole responsibility.

ISBN 978-1-967175-00-0
Ebook ISBN 978-1-967175-07-9

Library of Congress Control Number 2025035336

1 2 3 4 5 VERSA 30 29 28 27 26

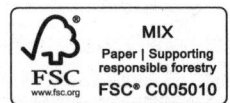

*To everyone around the world
doing what they can to keep
the spirit of democracy alive.*

With you I stand.

═CONTENTS═

PART 3: PRACTICE DEMOCRACY WITH HANDS AND HEART

═ INTRODUCTION ═

True Democracy Slumbers If We Do.
Let Us Be Awake!

> *We have frequently printed the word Democracy.*
> *Yet I cannot too often repeat that it is a word the real gist*
> *of which still sleeps, quite unawaken'd.*
>
> —WALT WHITMAN, *Democratic Vistas*

Consider this book a warm hug for weary hearts. It is written for caring people and compassionate citizens who want to stay engaged, who desire to do their part to make the world a better place, but who are exhausted by the unending rhetorical battle that democracy has become.

What passes for "democracy" today is anything but. We've been tricked into thinking democracy is a "war" between political parties for control over the levers of power, with everyday citizens like you and me expected to enlist in the "battle" to defeat our "enemies." Many politicians seem to care more about winning elections than the impacts of their policies or actions on our collective well-being. This model of democracy is not just ineffective and wrongheaded. It's destroying the human spirit, making us wary of our fellow citizens and compromising our capacity for wonder, belonging, mutual care, and shared joy.

The "real gist" of democracy is not combat. Democracy is a practice. It is something we do together, in community, with our friends, neighbors, colleagues, strangers, and yes, even supposed "foes," to care for each other and for the life we share. Democracy is rooted in habits of love, compassion, and gratitude—not in hatred, rage, or resentment. Yet it has begun to feel like we live at high noon, under a blood red sky, just waiting for catastrophe to strike. Standing on the edge like this takes a real toll on the mind, the body, and the spirit. Just because people disagree does not mean we cannot get along, or that we cannot work together to meet the challenges of the moment.

My friends, I say to you today that there is a way to disengage from the vitriol without opting out of society or becoming a hermit. There is a way to engage more skillfully with the world without being overwhelmed by the doom and gloom. There is a way to effect change without going to war, even as we uphold our deep moral commitments to each other and to the common goods we share. There is a way to disagree with others without demonizing them. There is a way to live so life doesn't feel like a battle. There is a way to be truly whole, safe, and at peace in this life, together.

The way is mindful democracy. And the first step is to declare our interdependence.

On July 4, 2026, Americans celebrate the 250th anniversary of the signing of the Declaration of Independence. Few documents have captured the world's imagination in the way this text has. In just 1,337 words, the Declaration announced the birth of a new nation in such inspiring and demonstrative terms that, in the ensuing centuries, dozens of nations modeled their own declarations of independence on it, as did the United Nations with its

Universal Declaration of Human Rights. Whenever anyone today determines to "declare independence" with a public pronouncement, it's almost certain they will echo words originally written in Philadelphia during the sweltering summer of 1776.

Though the Declaration of Independence was addressed to the "candid world," its true audience was everyday Americans. Its authors intended it to be read aloud, in bars, parks, churches, town halls, and military encampments, because these are the places where people gathered. The Declaration's authors aimed to inspire common folks to believe they deserved the "inalienable rights" of "life, liberty, and the pursuit of happiness" and to believe, as well, that these rights required standing up for themselves and embracing self-government. The Declaration's lasting power lies in its ability to inspire everyday people like you and me to believe that we matter, and that if we work together, we can build a world where everyone gets to enjoy the miracle of this life.

The semi-quincentennial celebration of the Declaration's signing is an auspicious moment to update this document to best suit the needs of *this* moment. We live today at a time of enemyship, with the political world fractured into "us versus them." So divided, we find it difficult to work together across our differences to care for the life we share—and so democracy continues to sleep. Enemyship is a cruel fiction: useful for justifying war, useless for democracy. The updated Declaration must transcend enemyship and remind us of the meaning of true democracy. The 2026 Declaration must focus on what we share and how deeply we are interconnected. It must recognize that democracy is not a war—in fact, the surest and quickest means to destroy democracy is to transform it into a war.

I've written a new Declaration of *Inter*dependence to begin this book. Like the original, it is 1,337 words long. If you agree to its principles, I invite you to sign your mark to it. It's printed on pages that can be torn out and carried with you; it's meant to be read aloud and discussed with friends and neighbors and strangers, and I hope that you will do so, on July 4 and on other days, too, in the United States and around the world. For if we are to stand up for true democracy—which I define as *working together to care for each other and for the life we share*—Americans alone cannot do it. A world divided against itself cannot, and will not, stand. The people and beings living on Planet Earth are interdependent and interconnected, today more than ever before, so we must speak up in all the world's languages and stand for democracy in all the world's climates.

To declare interdependence is to acknowledge and celebrate a basic and inescapable fact of human existence: each of us is interwoven with other people, other beings, and this beautiful blue orb we call home. Just as a wave would not exist without the ocean, a tree would not exist without the ground, and a gust of wind would not exist without the atmosphere, the same is true of humanity: none of us would exist without waves, trees, wind, apples, bees, oceans, words, farmers, scientists, a planet earth, a moon, a sun—and other people. Life is collaboration, not combat. This recognition is a natural insight of mindfulness, the practice of being aware of what is going on inside of and around us.

In my experience, mindfulness gives rise to a sense of connection and compassion that make it not only possible, but inevitable, that we will care for each other and protect the well-being of all who share this planet. Only when we awake to interdependence can we begin to practice true democracy, can we reliably choose to cooperate with each other rather than to compete or engage in combat. And if we do, we will be so much stronger and more capable. Whatever moxie, whatever gumption, whatever pluck, grit, and stick-to-itiveness we have when we act alone is multiplied exponentially when we work together as a community that bridges difference and division. Two people generally have more strength than one; consider the strength of three, or four, or dozens, or thousands, or millions! That's the true power of democracy, the power of cooperation and community, the power that comes from standing on common ground and declaring interdependence.

ON "MINDFUL DEMOCRACY"

When I speak in this book about "democracy," please make a distinction in your mind between what democracy once aspired to be and the farce "democracy" has become. Real democracy, true democracy, is not a war, and it is not something we do only on election days. It is not focused solely, or chiefly, on winning expensive political campaigns. True democracy is how everyday folks like you and me work together across disagreements and divisions to care for each other and for the life we share.

True democracy is "mindful democracy." I define "mindfulness" simply as *being aware of whatever is happening right here and right now.* "To meditate is to be aware of what is going on," Thich Nhat Hanh explains. Years of studying democracy as a scholar and teaching university students to be engaged citizens and ethical leaders has convinced me democracy does not work without mindfulness. Democracy demands the skills we learn by practicing meditation: paying attention, slowing down, pausing judgment, looking deeply, speaking lovingly, and listening carefully. In fact, I've come to think of mindfulness as a type of civic education. For democracy to regain its power to change lives and worlds, we the people must learn to live more mindfully.

Most of us have been conditioned since childhood to see the world in terms of friends and enemies. In the process, we've lost track of how deeply interconnected we truly are. A jewel of mindfulness practice is that it wakes us up to our interdependence, potentially correcting one of our culture's greatest blind spots. It's not enough to simply understand interdependence on an intellectual level. Mindfulness opens us to experiencing interdependence in an embodied way—yes, we understand in our minds that our fates are bound, but we also feel it in our hearts, see it in our breath, and hear it in our words. We recognize that life is not a zero-sum game in which your joy somehow diminishes mine, and that happiness is not an apple pie with a limited number of slices.

Mindfulness shows us we are not enemies. If you suffer less, I will suffer less, for you will be less likely to inflict your suffering on me. And if we suffer less, all of us suffer less, for we will be less likely to inflict our suffering on the world. All of us benefit when there is less suffering, and more joy, in the world.

We must wake up. The question is how.

There are many paths to experiencing and then embodying the insight of interdependence.

There is the path of religion—teachers of all the world's faiths attest to the truth of interdependence. Though religion has long been used to divide people, many of the world's saints and *bodhisattvas* proclaimed the highest fruit of religious devotion to be a deep and unshakable experience of unity. As the Catholic author and Trappist monk Thomas Merton wrote, "My dear brothers, we are already one. But we imagine that we are not. What we have to be is what we are."

There is the path of yoga—the "highest secret" of yoga, according to Krishna in the *Bhagavad Gita*, is "oneness," and the greatest cause of suffering is "duality delusion." When yogis say "namaste" to each other, they acknowledge the myriad ways we are interconnected.

There is the path of ecology. Study the generosity of green things, and the truth of interdependence becomes clear. As Robin Wall Kimmerer writes of the forest: "What happens to one happens to us all. We can starve together or feast together. All flourishing is mutual."

There is the path of science. In response to a rabbi struggling to comfort his nineteen-year-old daughter over the death of her sixteen-year-old sister, the physicist Albert Einstein wrote these poignant words:

> *A human being is a part of the whole, called by us "Universe,"
> a part limited in time and space. He experiences himself, his
> thoughts and feelings as something separated from the rest—a
> kind of optical delusion of his consciousness. This delusion is a
> kind of prison for us, restricting us to our personal desires and to
> affection for a few persons nearest to us. Our task must be to free
> ourselves from this prison by widening our circle of compassion to
> embrace all living creatures and the whole nature in its beauty.*

There are the paths of poetry, of painting, of photography, of music, of gardening, of tending bonsai, of history, of philosophy— and many paths I'm surely forgetting or that I haven't encountered. So many roads lead to the insight of interdependence. Perhaps all roads do, if you follow them long enough.

The path I have walked is the path of mindfulness. My steps toward embodied interdependence on this path have been influenced by many teachers and practices, and in particular by the mindfulness meditation practice and Engaged Zen Buddhism of Vietnamese monk, poet, and peace activist Thich Nhat Hanh (who his students simply call "Thầy," Vietnamese for "teacher"). Because mindfulness is the tradition I know best and have embodied in my life, it is the path to interdependence I present in this book.

Mindfulness is a buzzword in our culture. But what does it mean, really? What *is* mindfulness? First of all, *mindfulness is a practice*. It's something you do. No one else can do it for you. The practice of mindfulness is not fussy or overly complicated, yet it is rich and multilayered. The more you practice, the deeper your practice becomes. Mindfulness begins as a practice of learning *to pay attention* to whatever is happening in this moment. It's hard to effect any kind of real change, or to enjoy life, if we're unable to focus on what is happening. Practicing mindfulness builds the power of concentration; without this power, democracy does not work.

Once we have trained ourselves to pay attention, the practice of mindfulness turns toward *slowing down and looking deeply*. Focusing on an object—the breath, the body, our feelings, our thoughts, our perceptions—the mind starts to calm down, making it possible to look more closely at our lives and our world. A distracted mind is like a lake on a windy day—the waves roar, churning up the muck and making it impossible to see to the bottom of things. By focusing and stilling the mind, we're able to see clearly and gain profound insight into ourselves and this life.

Slow down, look deeply, and you will see that the world is constantly changing, and that it is changing together in a complex dance of individuals and ensembles where everything is affected by everything else—nothing is truly apart. Thầy coined the term "interbeing" to describe this reality. Interbeing, he said, means "coexistence," "mutual interdependence," and "this is because that is." To look deeply, mindfully, is to see, to feel, and to experience interbeing and interdependence.

HOW TO STAND UP FOR TRUE DEMOCRACY

The world needs a new declaration, a Declaration of Interdependence—and it needs people like you, dear reader, who are ready to declaim it from the hilltops. This book's purpose is to help you to declare your interdependence and then to bring this insight to life in the practice of mindful democracy.

The majority of the original 1776 Declaration of Independence consists of twenty-seven grievances against King George III, most of which establish a state of enemyship. Flipping the script from opposition to affirmation, the pages that follow this new Declaration of Interdependence contain twenty-seven "insights" on which mindful democracy rests.

Part 1, "Stand on a Strong Foundation," will show you how to practice mindfulness to gain insight into the reality of interdependence. In these pages, you'll begin to see yourself, other people, and your relationships in a new light. You will start to recognize yourself as a collaborator in a shared miracle, rather than a competitor or combatant stuck in a partisan war.

Part 2, "Walk the Path of Interdependence," will show you how to put your new insights into practice to build "beloved" communities. It is in beloved communities, a term popularized by Martin Luther King Jr. and Thich Nhat Hanh, that people learn the essential civic skills of democracy: how to talk, how to deliberate, and how to love and care for one another as kin. Without these skills, any stand for democracy is doomed.

Part 3, "Practice Democracy with Hands and Heart," will show you and the members of your community how to bring mindful democracy to life so we can care for each other and for the world we share. At a moment when so many people want to help but don't know what to do, this final section offers concrete actions to transcend enemyship and work together with others to build the type of world we'd like to inhabit.

We live in a culture that seems determined to get us down—on ourselves and on each other. Hope is in short supply. But even in moments of conflict, division, and great suffering, like this one, the conditions for transformation are also present. We already have the thing we most need to build a more loving and compassionate world: we have each other.

My friends, we are enemies only in our minds. In reality, we inter-are—we are all in this together. Our independence is also interdependence. To practice mindful democracy is to see a path toward ending the political war, and quieting the vituperation, so we can get down to the noble work that needs to be done: building a healthy world where everyone belongs, is safe, and can experience well-being, a meaningful world where everyone is free to answer life's ultimate questions in their own terms, a compassionate world where no one wastes away from want, when there is such abundance, a world where we have each other's backs, a world at peace with itself.

So, let's begin. Not perfectly, not all at once, but with heart and with hope, in whatever way we are able.

The good news is: we don't have to do it alone.

A DECLARATION OF INTERDEPENDENCE TO MEND A FRACTURED WORLD

When in the course of human events, it becomes necessary for the citizens of the world to take a stand and declare, in a multitude of voices and all the world's tongues, that enough is enough—no longer will we stand aside while careless people casually set the world on fire, no longer will we watch democracy be destroyed and the inherent dignity of millions be slandered, no longer will we tolerate cruel and unjust systems that put profits ahead of people and deny that life, every single life, is a miracle—dignity requires that these citizens declare the causes which impel them to make this stand despite the possibility that simply continuing to suffer these evils would be so much simpler.

We hold these truths to be self-evident: that all people are created equal and interdependent; that everyone—all races, genders, classes, sexual identities, religions, and nationalities—belongs, and can be truly well, and has something to contribute to the ensemble, and deserves the opportunity to answer life's ultimate questions in their own words; that in this endeavor life, liberty, and happiness are sacred; and that no one need waste away from want, when there is abundance. We stand on the common ground of our existence, aware that the present moment is the only moment that exists, the only moment in which change is possible. Friendship, not enemyship, is our foundation; affirmation, not destruction, is our politics; love, not hate, is our motivation; we act not for light and transient causes, but for the eternal aim: that we all might be truly whole, safe, and at peace in this life, together.

We stand for democracy. However, when a long train of abuses and usurpations so completely corrupts the meaning of *democracy* that the word itself becomes a contradiction, casually continuing to use that word is counterproductive. New clarity is called for. Contemporary democracy no longer serves to empower the multitudes; we the people must take it back. Let us stand for true democracy: the practice of caring for each other and for the life we share, where everyone has a say in decisions that affect their lives, and all of us pitch in to fix an injustice that affects us all. True democracy is collective empowerment: democracy not just *of*, *by*, or *for* the people, but also *with* the people, regardless of who they are.

Recognizing that there is no way to democracy because democracy is the way—we make this declaration to win hearts, not wars. We declare interdependence in the welcoming, compassionate spirit of beloved community, fully aware that the world we seek rests on the following insights:

✳ **We practice democracy** because we actively embrace life. Life is not a chore, a debt, an obligation, or something to be casually tossed aside with indifference. Life is a shared miracle.

✳ **Democracy is how we care** for each other and for the miraculous life that we share.

✳ **Democracy requires us to be present** with what is and see reality clearly, when it is joyful, and when it is painful. For this reason, we practice mindfulness of what is happening within and around us.

✳ **Democracy does not work without mindfulness.** We practice mindfulness to recover our agency as human beings, so that we can be more responsive and less reactive in how we live our lives.

✳ **It is natural to run away from suffering,** yet—like the lotus flower, which grows in the mud—we need suffering to bloom. . . .

✳ **And when we bloom, we bloom together.**

✳ **The present moment is a wonderful moment**—because it exists, because we are alive, and because we are capable of connection, community, and change.

✳ **Democracy requires us to show up for life,** and for each other—so we are mindful of how we use technology and what media we consume.

✳ **Even in moments of sorrow and grave injustice, the conditions for transformation are present**—the on-ramp to a better life is wherever you happen to be right now.

✳ **Gratitude is the foundational democratic emotion,** for it reconnects us to ourselves, to each other, and to the life we share.

✳ **Democracy requires us to open and strengthen our hearts** and to expand them to the size of infinity—for this reason, we practice loving-kindness.

✳ **Democracy starts when we stop living the lie** that some people are naturally more important and more deserving of safety, happiness, and well-being than other people.

✳ **Democracy is community,** and we make our community "beloved" by transforming it into a gymnasium where we practice mindful democracy and a microcosm of the world we'd like to create.

❋ **Democracy is a practice of inclusion,** for there is wisdom, creativity, and joy in diversity.

❋ **Every I is also a We;** instead of fighting with our fellow citizens, we learn from and support each other as we collaborate on common projects, challenges, and dreams.

❋ **The interdependence that demands conformity is not true interdependence:** it is tyranny.

❋ **The surest way to destroy democracy is to treat it like a war;** enemyship is easy, but it is to be avoided at all costs.

❋ **Democracy requires collaboration.** Whenever people work together, conflicts arise; when we disagree, it's skillful to treat others as "mistaken" rather than "evil."

❋ **Democratic power is not physical power:** it is not about domination; democratic power is spiritual power: it is the power we collectively generate from building safe, inclusive, and vibrant communities in which we care for each other and our shared life.

❋ **Mindful citizens care,** meaning we do not acquiesce to injustice or bow down to the status quo.

❋ **Democracy is about opening minds and hearts,** not winning wars. Democracy is not a battle between enemies; it is an argument between equals. When we speak and act, our aim is persuasion, not domination.

❋ **The skillful use of words is the cornerstone of democracy:** before we act, we deliberate.

✳ **Changing one's mind is not weakness**, it is the work of a brave soul.

✳ **The true power of words is to mend.**

✳ **Hatred has no place in democracy.**

✳ **It is a mark of wisdom to pause before acting** to ask, "Are you sure?"

✳ **When it's time, we act to affirm and to awaken,** not to denigrate or destroy.

Friends, let us heed these insights and join together in building communities of mutual support and transformation around the world so that we might work hand in hand to care for the life we share. Friends, we are enemies only in our minds, so let us mutually pledge to engage with the present moment—and all moments to come—in the spirit of collaboration rather than competition. Friends, we can change the world, so let us work together to alter the shared circumstances that cause all of us to suffer. Friends, if we see things clearly, there is always hope, so let us set out on a journey together, around the broad circle of the world, from now to next and encompassing all hours of the twenty-four, through night and day, through misery and joy, through unity and division, to experience a life whose true worth can never be calculated in dollars and cents, a life too valuable to be bought and sold, a life that is the greatest gift any of us will ever receive, a life meant to be treasured and enjoyed and never wasted, a life that is shared.

Our independence has always been *inter*dependence. Let us embrace it, declare it, and live by it, for the benefit of all beings.

I DECLARE INTERDEPENDENCE

If your heart recognizes these words as true—if you feel called to live by them—make your mark here. Print or sign your name. Press your fingerprint in the earth's mud. Draw a symbol that feels like you. However you choose, let this page bear witness to your promise: to live in alignment with life, with deep care and compassion for one another, and with the deep vow of democracy rooted in love.

_____   _____

NAME AND PLACE   DATE

TEAR HERE

STAND *on* COMMON GROUND

Democracy is a practice of standing on common ground. We are all in this together— not as comrades fighting a shared enemy, but as brothers and sisters living an interconnected, mutually supported life. We are united in our diversity, free even as we are bound to one another. In the following pages, I describe how to gain embodied insight into interdependence by practicing mindfulness, and how to orient your mindfulness practice toward the goals of democracy: caring for each other and for our shared life.

LIFE IS A MIRACLE— AND IT IS SHARED

Life is not a chore, a debt, an obligation,
or something to be casually tossed aside
with indifference. Life is a shared miracle.
We practice democracy because we actively
embrace life, and the people in it.

Life is a miracle. It is awesome, wonderful, mysterious, beyond explanation. Its value can never be calculated in dollars. It is too valuable to be bought and sold. It is the greatest gift, something to be treasured and never wasted. It deserves all our attention.

The practice of mindfulness reveals that life is a miracle—and that this miracle is shared.

In his touchstone 1975 book *The Miracle of Mindfulness*, a work that introduced many Westerners to mindfulness, the Zen Buddhist teacher Thich Nhat Hanh observed the beauty of a mindfulness practice: in a world of distraction and disinterest, practicing mindfulness draws attention to the everyday miracle of being alive. "People usually consider walking on water or in thin air a miracle. But I think the real miracle is to walk on earth," he wrote. "Every day we are engaged in a miracle we don't even recognize: a blue sky, white clouds, green leaves, the black, curious eyes of a child—our own two eyes. All is a miracle."

It took four-and-a-half billion years for each of us to wake up this morning. Life will never be the same once you see this miracle. Perhaps many things that seemed important no longer will. Things you once ignored may now feel the most meaningful. This breath, this body, simply being here at all right now—miracles. It's a miracle how perfectly our lungs fit into our chests, nestled up against our hearts. It's a miracle, too, how perfectly we are adapted to this planet, nestled the ideal distance from the sun, and to this atmosphere, created by trees and other green things.

Look deeply, and you'll see these miracles are shared. Our bodies are fashioned out of earth and sky and wind and fire and stardust. Our breath is the wind that rings the hot equator, our blood the world's waves and rivers, our bodies its mountains and soils, our voices the sound of people singing in all the world's languages. Our lives are the gentle arc of the sun rising over the horizon and sinking back again. We are waves that would not exist without the ocean.

Look deeply, and you'll see how many things had to happen just as they did for billions of years for this moment to exist and for you to be reading these words. Think of all our ancestors had to do, and the pure luck they must have experienced, so each of us could be here today. Think of how the stars had to align! Had just one of our ancestors slipped and fallen down a cliff or been eaten by a tiger before their children were conceived, we wouldn't be here today, and the world would be different.

Every day we speak languages we did not invent, walk on paths we did not pave, mostly eat food we did not grow, write on devices we did not build, and connect over an internet most of us did not create. We are who we are because of our own efforts as well as the efforts of our ancestors, our families, our mentors, our teachers, our communities, and our friends. There is no me and no you without the earth that is our home and our common ground. After all, as I often remind my students, trees and lungs have the same shape. There is no me and no you without the plants we eat, the cooling rains that become the rivers and lakes we drink, the trees that purify the air we breathe, the bacteria that colonize our bellies and digest our food for us, or the antibodies that fight off disease and cancer. There is no me and no you without us.

Our lives are a miracle, a miracle we share with others. To be alive is to set out on a journey said in many cultures to be solitary but that is, in fact, shared. We share the miracle, the path, and the practice. Other people, and other beings, play a significant role in making our miraculous lives possible. Truly, our being is interbeing.

Behold the shared miracle in every person, in every object, in every hour of the twenty-four, and in each moment, and you take a step along the path of democracy—for democracy is how we protect and nourish the miracle of simply being alive.

DEMOCRACY IS HOW WE CARE *for* EACH OTHER AND *for* THE LIFE WE SHARE

Democracy is a practice of caring
for the shared miracle we call life,
in all its joyfulness and all its pain.

Democracy is not a war. Democracy is not a competition. Democracy is not a battle between political parties for votes, attention, and money. Democracy is an on-going practice of taking care of each other, and of this miraculous, messy, wonderful, perplexing, oft-challenging life we share.

Slow down, and look deeply, and you'll discover an inescapable fact of being human: everyone hurts, sometimes. Life has many joys. There is also suffering in life. And this suffering invites care. To care is to alleviate suffering.

Look even more deeply, and you will see not all suffering is the same. There are at least two kinds of suffering. First, there is the pain innate to the human condition: sickness, old age, and death. Second, there is hurt created and amplified by humans. This second kind of suffering includes the wasting plagues we inflict upon each other—enemyship, war, discrimination, dehumanization, racism, sexism, homophobia, colonialism, animal abuse, and environmental destruction, to name just a few—as well as the suffering we inflict on ourselves: self-judgment, holding onto a grudge, contemplating revenge on an enemy, worrying about things we can't change, or consuming in ways that don't support our well-being, for example.

As skilled as we are in the arts of friendship, we are equally skilled in the arts of enemyship: in transforming life into a battle between an us and a them. People build monuments to heaven and caste systems that reduce people's lives to hell. Humans are particularly gifted at drawing lines and building walls. From a young age, we are taught to mark some lives as superior, others as inferior, and, even worse, still others as irrelevant and even disposable. Recognizing this, authoritarian leaders determined to destroy democracy demonize immigrants, foreigners, and people who look and sound different from themselves as "criminals," "lowlifes," "animals," and "barbarians." One of the greatest insults in the human vocabulary is to say this or that person is "nothing." Yet people say it all the time.

Let's call the first kind of inevitable suffering "sorrow," and the second kind of artificial hurt, particularly the kind we inflict on each other rather than on ourselves, "injustice." Of course, these two forms of pain compound each other. It's not always easy to disentangle them.

As long as we are human, there will be sorrow. Caring citizens are doing important work and research to advance our knowledge into healthy living every day, and we know of many things we can do to mitigate sickness. We can (sometimes) live in a healthy environment with clean water and air, medicine, and good healthcare. If we choose to stay active, eat well, sleep, take time to do things that nourish the spirit, and build community, we can increase the quality of our lives and the likelihood of aging well. That said, sometimes we cannot control the quality of the air we breathe or the food we eat. In the end, we cannot transcend sickness, old age, and death. The practice of mindfulness aims to transform our relationship to sorrow so it doesn't hurt so much or cause us to lash out at others.

It's true that we will never fully transcend sickness, old age, and death, nor will we ever completely eliminate human bias or error. Still, we can take care of the suffering we inflict upon ourselves with our thoughts and choices. Such suffering makes life seem less than a miracle. And, if we learn to work together in community while standing on common ground, we *can* end many forms of injustice. We can alleviate the human-caused suffering we inflict on each other—and that, my friends, is a goal of true democracy. Democracy is a communal practice of working together to care for ourselves, each other, and the world we share. When we practice democracy together, we aim to reduce the amount of suffering in the world and to ensure everyone is supported, safe, and has enough to live a good life as they choose to define it.

Having enemies is one of the main reasons human beings suffer. Today we suffer the agony of "duelity," a life of false binaries experienced as duels between enemies. There is nothing inevitable about the enemyships that fuel racism or sexism or war or poverty or environmental destruction. There is nothing invincible about these forms of injustice, either.

Practicing mindfulness to gain insight into the reality of interbeing and awaken to the shared miracle we call life, we see the injustices that cause us the most pain are shared with others. Many people are affected by foul air, fetid water, poverty, the inability to find a meaningful job, discrimination, racism, sexism, ableism, xenophobia, environmental destruction, rising seas, wildfires, imperialism, neoliberalism, war, and violence. If we are going to be safe and happy and free and at peace, we must be safe and happy and free and at peace together. When it comes to our shared miracle life, we are not enemies at all. We are collaborators bonded together in a pact of mutual care.

The causes of our suffering are shared, because life is shared. That means the remedies are shared, too. When the causes of our suffering are too big for any of us to manage as individuals, we must work together with others to find the happiness, freedom, and peace we seek. Mindfulness begins with the individual, and taking care of our own suffering is the fertile soil that allows care for our fellow humans to grow. Yet as the practice develops, it becomes communal. We explore mindfulness alongside others to learn how to live and work together. Mindfulness is democracy's foundation.

IN A DISTRACTED WORLD, BEING PRESENT IS REVOLUTIONARY

As mindfulness has exploded in popularity, it's important to consider why we practice. The practice is not about being more productive at work, and it's not just about relaxation, either. It is definitely not about becoming better adjusted to a poisonous society. We practice mindfulness to see reality clearly and be present with what is so we can better care for ourselves, for each other, and for our shared life.

No one enjoys feeling distracted, off-kilter, and out of sorts—or out of time. It's no surprise, then, that mindfulness has become one of the world's most popular meditation practices over the past forty years.

If you haven't practiced mindfulness yet, there are many wonderful resources to get you started. When I teach mindfulness to my university students, we work through Mark Williams and Danny Penman's *Mindfulness: An 8-Week Plan for Finding Peace in a Frantic World*, which is based on the authors' research at Oxford University. When I teach mindfulness in our community *sangha* (meditation group), we work through Thich Nhat Hanh's *The Mindfulness Survival Kit: Five Essential Practices*. Thich Nhat Hanh's Plum Village community's amazing, free meditation app is unmatched in terms of the quality of the meditations available. Tara Brach's "R.A.I.N" practice (recognize, allow, investigate, nurture) and Rhonda Magee's "S.T.O.P." practice (stop, take a deep breath, observe, proceed) are simple and profound techniques that easily can be integrated into your daily life. Podcasts are also a great place to start—I highly recommend Plum Village's podcast *The Way Out is In*, cohosted by Jo Confino and Brother Phap Huu, and Dan Harris's *10% Happier* podcast. Krista Tippett has hosted many memorable conversations about meditation on her podcast *On Being* (my favorite podcast of all time, and one of our culture's greatest treasures). If you ask around, I bet there are fantastic meditation teachers and communities of practice nearby who would happily support your practice!

As you get started—and as you continue—I urge you to contemplate why we practice mindfulness in the first place, *and* why we don't. . . .

For mindfulness's explosion of popularity has come at a cost.

As a result of extensive research into meditation's many health benefits—it reduces stress and anxiety, promotes better sleep, helps healing after injury and illness, and allows us to feel more at home in our bodies and in our lives—mindfulness is now practiced in elementary schools, government offices, professional sports, boardrooms, prisons, police departments, and the military. Popular apps such as Headspace, Calm, and Insight Timer make it easy for anyone to access guided meditations—just plug in your headphones and hit play.

Businesses and corporations have taken note and often advise their workers to practice mindfulness to be more productive. Mindfulness has become so business-friendly that it has been called a new "capitalist spirituality," or, more ironically, "McMindfulness." What originated as a Buddhist practice for relieving suffering has been secularized and reframed as a modern scientific discipline with very little connection to its roots.

One does not have to be a Buddhist to practice or benefit from mindfulness. The "Buddha" (translated as "the awakened one") himself was clear on this point. He did not say, "Believe this (or believe me) and it will set you free;" he said, "Try this practice out and see if it helps." He shared his teachings with anyone who asked, no matter their religion, caste, gender, or age. He did not discriminate between worthy and unworthy or friends and enemies. He taught kings and peasants and criminals. Unlike many yoga and meditation gurus of his time, he refused to reserve "the good stuff" for only his most senior students, or for the rich and well-connected who could offer him the most gold. He taught anyone and everyone. The Buddha hoped that all people, Buddhist or not, would take something useful from his experience.

The Buddha was not a god, nor did he pretend to be. He was a person named Siddhartha Gautama who spent most of his life in what is now Northern India and Southern Nepal from approximately 563 to 483 BCE. The Buddha devoted his life to meditation, seeking a cure for suffering. In recognizing that there is inevitable suffering and there is suffering we cause ourselves and others (what I've called "sorrow" and "injustice"), his studies and practice led him to the insight of interdependence. With this liberating insight, the Buddha dedicated himself to teaching others how to experience freedom from the suffering we cause, too. His message was revolutionary and radically democratic.

Today it seems like mindfulness is everywhere, and everyone is doing it. Most people who practice mindfulness do it for stress relief and relaxation, to feel more at home in their bodies, and to be better able to meet the demands of a world that asks so much of us. For many, mindfulness is a coping mechanism to better navigate an unbalanced, fractured, often unjust world. By making mindfulness as secular and scientific as possible, contemporary scientists and doctors and teachers have made it possible for this practice to reach a wide audience who need it. That is a very good thing.

However, as mindfulness has become more popular, the purpose of the practice has often changed from liberation to adjustment, from radical transformation to stress relief. Because the *why* of mindfulness has become different, what people learn about the practice itself has changed; in the process, much of the wisdom that informed mindfulness for millennia has gone missing.

Though you don't have to be a Buddhist to practice mindfulness, it is illuminating to consider why many Buddhists practice mindfulness—and to consider what you can learn from them. For the engaged Buddhists I know, the practice is not about being more productive at work, and it's not just about relaxation, either. It is definitely not about becoming better adjusted to a poisonous society. The point is not to feel better for a time, and then to keep living our lives just as we have before without changing the habits that cause us pain. For engaged Buddhists, the point is to transform how we live in the world, so that we suffer less and inflict less suffering on others, and then to build engaged communities that are capable of transforming the world itself, making it a less painful and a more caring place, for one and all.

Mindfulness, though not strictly a means to an end, tends to transform ourselves and the world—because in a distracted, off-kilter world, the simple act of being present is a revolution. If you are fully present, if you look deeply and see that life is a shared miracle unfolding on (and through) common ground, this insight will change your life, if you allow it to. Because once you've glimpsed the true nature of things, once you've seen the miracle in all its majesty and mystery, you can no longer fiddle contentedly while the world burns. Insight into interdependence reveals that when the world burns, you and I burn, too. To take care of ourselves means taking care of the world, because the world is us. Sitting on the sidelines is no longer an option, not that it ever truly was.

Once you see things clearly, as an interdependent, interconnected whole, life is not the same—and neither is our understanding of democracy. Life is not a war, and neither is democracy. Democracy is a practice of mutual care. In collaboration, we can make life more joyful and less painful, for ourselves, for other people, and for all beings.

Keep this in mind as you practice: mindfulness might be quiet and peaceful, but it also can be revolutionary. The insights that arise when you become increasingly aware of what is going on inside of and around you, and the way these insights live in your body, might change the very way you move through the world.

Don't be surprised if the path of mindfulness also leads you to democracy.

DEMOCRACY DOES NOT WORK *without* MINDFULNESS

Democracy does not work without mindfulness, for it requires us to be present, to see things clearly, and to refuse to continue to blindly repeat the errors of the past. We practice mindfulness to recover our agency as human beings so we can be more responsive and less reactive in how we live our lives.

The practice of mindfulness is based on an insight first described by ancient meditators: human beings have the capacity to observe experience without getting tangled up in it. This means, simply and wonderfully, it is possible to observe ourselves having a craving, or a happy thought, or even a scary emotion, without amplifying those feelings or sending our minds spiraling off into rumination about old memories or fretful anticipation of future events.

Practicing mindfulness, we can observe ourselves having an experience without immediately reacting to that experience. We can see it might not be necessary to layer story after story on top of emotion in a way that feeds the craving, the joy, the doubt, or the fright until it overwhelms us. Watching thoughts and emotions come and go without immediately reacting to them, it becomes possible to make choices about how we want to respond—and to decide more deliberately how we want to live our lives.

Mindfulness is how we recover our agency as human beings— and this is another reason why democracy does not work without mindfulness. Mindfulness is how we keep from being overwhelmed, or at least from feeling overwhelmed about being overwhelmed. Mindfulness is how we reclaim the ability to make deliberate, considered choices about how we engage with life and with challenges.

Practicing mindfulness, we learn to be fully present with whatever is happening right now. Often, what is happening is suffering—ours, and others'. If we can learn to be with our own suffering without letting it overwhelm us or responding violently to it, we can show up for life in all its ups and downs. With practice, we may no longer feel the need to run away from our suffering, or from the suffering of others, whether it comes in the inevitable form of sorrow or the human-caused form of injustice. We may see suffering clearly—see that it has causes and conditions, that it is shared.

Once we recover our agency, we can engage in the world without adding more suffering to it. With a strong foundation of mindfulness, we can open ourselves to the deep emotion of our many challenges without dropping out or turning away in overwhelm. By learning to practice democracy, to be and work together in community, we can find refuge and joy in a world on fire where it is not just the temperature that is rising, but also people's tempers. Practicing mindful democracy, we can learn to take care of our own suffering and then, if we can be with the suffering of others without it overwhelming us, or without adding our suffering to theirs, we can show up for each other. We can build community, pledge to support each other, and work together to change the world by altering the shared circumstances that cause all of us to suffer.

Recovering our agency does not automatically change the world. It is but a step on the path to change—though a necessary one. When it comes to real change, thoughts and prayers are not enough. We will not change the world by wanting and wishing. But the mindfulness that offers us embodied insight into our interconnection increases the chances we will see what needs to be done and be able to do it without accidentally making things worse.

The small moments of peace you feel in your mindfulness practice, moments when you have an experience but do not immediately react to it or get lost in it, might seem inconsequential when compared to the multilayered suffering of the world. But take heart—the seed of real change is found in these moments. These mindful moments make it possible to show up for the miracle and to see life more clearly; without them, democracy and lasting change are impossible.

THERE IS NO LOTUS *without* MUD

It is natural to try to run away
from suffering, yet—like the lotus flower,
which grows in the mud—we need
suffering to bloom.

In the Plum Village meditation tradition, we have a saying: "No mud, no lotus." The lotus flower is a symbol of enlightenment. This beautiful flower roots in mud and rises through murky waters in search of light—just like us. It's easy to get stuck in the mud, to be mired in the darkness of fear and frustration and hate and division. Unfortunately, mud is like quicksand: the more you struggle against it, the deeper you sink.

In the ancient Indian language of Pali, the language of many Buddhist texts, the word now translated into English as "mindfulness" is *sati*, which is closely related to the verb *sarati*, "to remember."* Surprisingly, one meaning of mindfulness is remembering. Mindful remembering does not mean dwelling on the past or ruminating over bygone events. It means "remembering to come back to the present moment." It also means remembering the insights we've gained from our practice, remembering with each breath that we are connected to the beings around us and the earth itself. With mindfulness, we re-member ourselves as an essential part of an interwoven whole.

Always remember: no mud, no lotus. Without mud, without sorrow, without hurt, there would be no reason to seek light. Consider: a person experiences neck and back pain (mud); it inspires them to seek out a yoga practice that heals their injuries (lotus). A person is diagnosed with high blood pressure (mud); it encourages them to adopt a healthier diet and workout regimen (lotus). A person feels great stress and anxiety doomscrolling through the news (mud); it persuades them to practice mindfulness (lotus).

---

*In Sanskrit, the cognate word to the Pali "sati" that is now translated into English as "mindfulness" is the word "smṛti" (स्मृति), which means "that which is remembered." It was the scholar Thomas William Rhys Davids in 1881 who first translated "sati" into English as "mindfulness," rendering "samma-sati" as "Right Mindfulness: the active, watchful mind." Buddhist Suttas, Volume 11 of The Sacred Books of the East, ed. F. Max Müller (Oxford: Clarendon Press, 1881), 107.

A person suffers from feelings of loneliness and powerlessness, despairing that nothing they do ever makes the world a better place (mud); they gather with others and build a community (lotus). A community frets that democracy has become a perpetual war that adds to rather than soothes our suffering (mud); that community begins to practice true democracy—and everything changes (lotus).

To practice mindfulness is to follow the example of the lotus. We find light not by denying that mud exists, not by cursing it or waging war on it. We use it to grow. Then we figure out how to grow and blossom together. Without mud, there would be no lotus. Without suffering, we would not be motivated to change.

In Vietnam, myriad little lakes have formed from bomb craters. Lotus flowers now grow in these lakes. I saw these lakes with my own eyes on a pilgrimage to visit Thich Nhat Hanh's root temple in Huế, and the images stick with me to this day. On a bus back to our hotel after seeing one of these lakes for the first time, I wrote this poem:

A Lotus for You

On a muddy lake in Vietnam a lotus blooms.
Who would suspect that flower was once a bomb,
dropped out of fear,
and misunderstanding, by
people who forgot that life is shared,
who saw numbers not faces,
who mistook destruction for justice?
Does the lotus remember being a bomb?
Does it care?
It smiles just the same.
I think the lotus remembers, and it takes special delight
in transforming ugliness into beauty.
I think the lotus is friends with the mud.

Lotus flowers grow from the mud. There is a lot of mud right now. The question is, what will we grow? How will we relate to this mud? What will we grow from the mud we all share? And how will we do this together?

LOTUS FLOWERS DO NOT GROW ALONE

When we bloom,
we bloom together.

Democracy emerges from the tender, honest, at times frustrating insight that our power to address injustice as individuals is severely limited—we need others to live and to live well. Hard work is a virtue, but individual initiative can only take us so far if we want to make the world a more peaceful, less painful place. It is only by joining with others that we can "change the world," by which I mean *change the shared circumstances that cause us all to suffer.*

Practicing mindfulness opens the doors to democracy. We must build strong, compassionate, loving communities that empower us to work together to reduce the suffering in the world. Mindful people are committed to acting in coordination with multitudes. Our challenge is to learn how to become a community of lotus flowers, in contact with mud and blooming together.

Lotus flowers do not grow alone. They grow in communities atop the water, spreading through rhizomes in the mud and seeds on the wind. Lotus flowers growing in the same pond share the same air, the same sunlight, and the same mud. It's common when practicing meditation to focus on our personal mud. Every autobiography is a story of joy and pain. And yet, when we become hyper-focused on the twists and turns of our own narrative, it becomes easy to overlook how much of our story is shared with other people, how much of our sorrow and suffering is intimately known by others in their own lives. Often, it is a feeling of isolation or victimization that compounds our suffering. Knowing we are not the only ones to feel the way we sometimes do can be a potent balm.

The Plum Village tradition often reminds us to "make good use of your suffering." Everyone knows how to make bad use of their suffering. Contemporary politics shows us how: blame other people for your pain and go to war against them, believing, wrongly, that their defeat will make us suffer less. This is not a good use of suffering, for it turns me against you and us against them. Fighting political wars solves nothing; it only makes our collective suffering more intense.

Can our suffering turn us toward others, opening us to connection, collaboration, and cooperation? If so, happiness is in reach. Look at how much we share, dear friends! We share the same mud. Our hearts hurt in remarkably similar ways. We also share the same light.

THE PRESENT MOMENT IS A WONDERFUL MOMENT

The present moment is a wonderful moment:
because it exists, because we are alive, and
because we are capable of connection,
community, and change.

There are plenty of reasons why the present moment is wonderful. The most obvious is that we are alive. The present moment is a wonderful moment simply because it exists and because we exist. The present moment is the miracle in which all other miracles unfold.

In the Plum Village tradition, when we practice mindful breathing, we have a saying:

> *Breathing in, there is only the present moment.*
> *Breathing out, it is a wonderful moment.*

This is also a core mantra of mindful democracy.

The present moment is the only moment because the past is gone, and the future hasn't happened yet. Life is lived in the present. The present is the only moment in which we have any control, agency, or freedom. The choices we make in the present affect the future, and all that is to come.

It's impossible to change the past; all we can do is try to see it clearly and do our best to understand it. The future hasn't happened yet—and it is so much bigger than any of us individually. As hard as we might try to influence the future, we can never completely foil fate. Our efforts are met at every turn by luck and chance and pure randomness, making life all the more sweet and, yes, also a touch bittersweet.

But the present? The present is alive with possibility. The present is the space of creativity and change. The present is the moment in which we recover our human agency.

Becoming skilled at mindfulness practice involves noticing how the past shapes and guides the present—the past is the mud from which the lotus grows. Awake to this reality instead of reacting to whatever happens just as we always have, we can deliberately choose to respond differently. Every time we do, we change the present—and the future. If we hope to change future moments, we must change how we live right now in the present. Our present conduct shapes what is and what is to come, so it is the most important thing.

The past is the present arrived.

The present is the space of freedom.

The future is the present to come.

The present moment is wonderful because it can be a mindful moment. Every person has the capacity for mindfulness. Being able to see our suffering clearly, understand it, and transform it makes life worth living.

The present moment is wonderful because we can touch reality—we can fully experience a blue sky, a sunset, a child's smile, the purr of a kitten. The present moment is wonderful because we can nourish the object of our attention. We can listen to our grandparents, to the children who live next door, to our beloveds, and make them feel heard. We can brighten someone's day in an elevator or in a grocery store with a smile, a kind word, or a joke. We can inspire a community that has lost its way to find refuge in each other and in the greater web that holds us all.

The present moment is wonderful because we can relieve another person's suffering, and our own. Healing words are among the greatest powers humans possess. The present moment is wonderful because, though there is suffering in life, we are not condemned to a life of pain. We already have the tools we need to begin transforming suffering into well-being, freedom, and happiness.

The present moment is wonderful because we are not alone. We are made of the world, made of each other. Humans have always collaborated. Democracy is community life, and democracy is part of our heritage—humans are communal beings.

The present moment is wonderful because there is hope. Hope is not false, nor is it idle. For centuries, dedicated meditators have transformed their sorrow and worked together to address injustice. These people were just like us. If they could do it then, we can do it now.

The present moment is wonderful because when we are fully awake to it, we can extend a hand. We can build community. We can practice democracy.

WHAT WE PAY ATTENTION *to* MATTERS

Democracy requires us to
show up for life, and for each other—
so we are mindful of how we use technology
and what media we consume.

Living in a world shaped by technology, today we need mind-fulness—the ability to be aware of and present with whatever is happening inside of and around us—more than ever. If we're not deliberate about how we use this technology, it can easily become a source of suffering in our lives that drives a wedge between us and other people.

Make no mistake: our technological devices are useful, and for many of us they have become necessary to function. Many of us need our phones to enter our houses and gyms and the buildings where we work, to board buses and planes, to operate our cars, to borrow books from the local library, and to check out at the grocery store. Social media allows us to connect to distant friends and family members, sometimes providing a much-needed life-line when we're lonely or need help. Social media also lets us know about meetings and demonstrations and other possibilities to come together in democratic action. We use apps to call for rides, to chat with friends halfway across the world, to practice medita-tion, to check the weather, and to find healthy places to eat when traveling. Technology has become a part of how we live, and that is not likely to change.

We must be careful, though, because the technology we have warmly embraced is part of what scholar and artist Jenny Odell calls an "attention economy." Most of the apps and platforms we use are controlled by large, multinational corporations—as you might guess, their motivation is profit above all else. The tech-nological revolution of mobile phones and watches, social media, and AI algorithms has made it possible for these corporations to reach us with content that can capture and monetize our focus at any moment, every day, no matter where we happen to be. This technology is designed to be addictive and to monopolize our attention. And this has fundamentally changed how we relate to other people and to democracy.

Have you ever tried to have a conversation with someone, but found it difficult to get *and to hold* their attention because they were so focused on their phone? Have you been the one with your head stuck in the phone? Every time we gather with others, we have an opportunity to connect—to look in another person's eyes, to speak from the heart, and to really hear what others say. Today we miss so many chances for genuine human connection. The next time you go out to a restaurant, take a look at the people around you. How many are making eye-contact and genuinely connecting with their companions? How many of them are looking at their phones instead of the people they are dining with?

We are what we consume, whether it's the food that becomes our cells, the air that moves our bodies, or the content that forms our consciousness. Do you find that engaging with the attention economy actually makes you feel worse? That's by design. Social media algorithms tend to promote hateful, outrageous, divisive, frightening content, because such content is addictive. The attention economy wants us to be overwhelmed because, in our discombobulation, we will turn to social media to seek comfort that might never come. The worse we feel, the better it is for the attention economy. The needy little devices most of us carry in our pockets and wear on our wrists, their apps incessantly beeping and buzzing and chirping at us all hours of the day, are designed to make us feel anxious and afraid and alone. Anxious we'll miss out on something important if we put our phones away. Afraid something bad is going to happen, so we stay tuned in just in case. Alone, and in need of comfort from some new toy.

The deeper we fall down the rabbit hole, the better it is for multinational corporations, but the worse it tends to be for us. Anxious, afraid, and alone, we start to lose all sense of time, perspective, purpose . . . and shared humanity. Democracy requires us to show up for life—and for each other. To do this, we must become more mindful about how we use technology. We must learn to be present with interdependence without turning against our fellow beings or running away.

The content we consume matters as much as when and how we consume it. In mindfulness practice, we see how what we choose to be mindful of matters—for we absorb the qualities of these objects in our consciousness. What we consume, and how we consume it, affects our minds, our bodies, and our spirit.

This means not all mindfulness is the same. While mindfulness, at its most fundamental, is a practice of paying attention, most Buddhist teachers say there are right and wrong ways to practice mindfulness. These dualistic labels of "right" and "wrong" are rooted in the impact your mindfulness practice has on your experience of suffering and stability. Right mindfulness leads to wholesomeness and health. Right mindfulness creates a deep and moving sense of connection to the present moment, and to your fellow human beings. It allows you to feel stability even in the midst of crisis. Wrong mindfulness—paying attention to things that destabilize you—makes it harder to live with embodied wisdom and compassion when, inevitably, challenges and sorrows arise.

* Does the content you consume encourage you to turn your back on life and your fellows?

* Does it trick you into seeing the world as it is not—as a theater of war, rather than an ongoing collaboration?

✳ Does it create the impression that it's impossible to get along with people with whom you disagree?

✳ Does it cause you to see red and to hear the drums of battle every time you disagree with someone?

✳ Does it downgrade or downplay the miracle of life?

✳ Does it suggest life is all mud and no light?

✳ Does it hold that *this* people—because of their skin color or religion or where they were born—are better than *that* people—because of their skin color or religion or where they were born?

✳ Does it say you are powerless and alone?

✳ Does it sow seeds of hatred, exclusion, and discrimination?

✳ Does it call on you to disparage, demean, and kill other beings?

✳ Does it make you so despondent that you can't turn away from it, or choose when to think about it and when to let it go?

✳ Does it encourage you to be a careless person who thinks more about money than the well-being of other people?

If you answered "yes" to any of these questions, you might be practicing wrong mindfulness. And if you answered "yes" to any of these questions, please know you're not alone. Wrong mindfulness is what the addictive algorithms of the attention economy are designed to make us practice.

What can you do to alleviate the suffering caused by wrong mindfulness? Let's be realistic here: I don't think the answer is to just ditch our devices. They are useful and essential tools, but often we use them in ways neither useful nor essential. It's not realistic to ban our devices from most spaces where we gather. Rather than running way from the attention economy, it's time for us to take back our agency by practicing mindfulness and becoming more deliberate about our technology use.

A good place to start is by noticing how your engagement with technology feels in your body. If you become more aware of how your media consumption impacts you, you can make more informed choices about how you engage with it—and how you want to proceed. Can you notice your lived, embodied sensations when you're on your devices? What happens to your breath, to your posture, to the position of your spine? Do you find yourself unconsciously clenching the muscles in your neck and jaws and feet? Do your eyes become teary or your vision blurry? Do you hold your breath, forgetting to breathe? Does your head hurt or your heart ache?

If you find that social media causes you bodily pain, it's impacting your spirit, too. When your body tightens and constricts, it's time to take a break. It's time to remember to come back to the present moment.

Most people could be more mindful about when they pick up their phones or check their smartwatches. If your unconscious habit is to reach for your phone first thing in the morning, or last thing before bed, try doing something different. When you wake, give yourself some time to really wake up and embrace the miracle of the day—to drink your tea or to stand outside or just to sit in mindfulness meditation. Set the tone for the day, rather than having it set for you by an algorithm. The same goes for bedtime—take some time to unplug so dreaming does not become an exercise in doomscrolling.

A few other suggestions: try disabling news notifications on your phone or watch. This will allow you to be more intentional about the news you read, where that news comes from, and when you read it. Recalibrate your news consumption. Can you pay just enough attention to what's going on in the news to be aware of the injustices that need addressing, but not so much attention that you drown in the flood of negativity? Can you balance your media consumption so it's not all doom?

Practice putting your phone away during important conversations, or when eating dinner, walking through nature, playing with your children, or doing yoga. Rather than mindlessly picking up your phone, do so deliberately. Make the conscious choice to engage and say to yourself: for the next few minutes, I will mindfully explore social media. As you do, set an alarm (a mindfulness bell) on your phone for a set time (five or ten minutes) as a reminder to come back to the present moment. Listen to your body and thoughts—if you find yourself overwhelmed, take breaks to breathe mindfully, to look out a window, to stand up, go for a mindful walk, or to talk with a friend.

These are likely not new ideas, but perhaps the time has come for you to cultivate some of them so you can show up for life, and for the people and creatures in yours. Reality is constantly happening, even if you don't take a picture of it to post online. Small moments of connection in real life are more miraculous than anything happening on your phone.

THE ON-RAMP IS WHEREVER YOU ARE NOW

Each of us matters—as individuals, and as a community. There is no reason to throw up your hands and say enough is enough; even in moments of pain, the conditions for transformation are present. The path to a more joyful and more connected life begins wherever you happen to be right now.

The voices of nihilism, of nothing-really-matters-ness, are strong in our culture. In dark moments, we may hear the chant of three nothings: you are nothing, nothing is real, nothing really matters. If we repeat this chant to ourselves, the flowers we could grow—sunnies, lotuses, columbines—begin to wilt.

Have you ever doubted your self-worth? Have you ever questioned if you matter? Please know you are not alone in having these thoughts. And please know that you, and your life, matter. I say this without hesitation or equivocation. How do I know? The proof is in the practice of mindfulness itself.

Your life matters because you are capable of pausing, of slowing down the fluctuations of your mind, and of looking deeply at your life as it is happening right now—and then choosing how to respond. You matter because you can cultivate and grow the best parts of yourself, the deepest parts of your unrealized goodness, to bring heartfelt presence and gladness into the world. You matter, and I matter, because we can respond to life with compassion and trust, even when we are in pain. We are not at the mercy of suffering. You matter, and I matter, because we can choose to engage wisely. We can learn how to pause, to step back from our immediate reactions, to see things clearly, and to make choices about how we want to live and be. Each and every one of us impacts the world in large and small ways with everything we do.

The first noble truth taught by the Buddha is *sarvam dukkham*: there is suffering in life. This truth has come to represent all of Buddhism, leading some to wrongly see it as a downhearted, depressing, nihilistic tradition. It's not. Buddhism is deeply, profoundly optimistic: yes, there is suffering in life, but it's possible to understand and transform it so we can be truly free. There are four noble truths, not one: (1) There is suffering in life; (2) There are causes of suffering; (3) Suffering can be overcome; (4) There is a path to overcoming suffering, the noble eightfold path.

For Buddhists, right mindfulness means talk of suffering must be accompanied by talk of its transformation. This becomes clear when we consider the word itself. The ancient Pali word for suffering, *dukkha*, is a metaphor for a bumpy ride. *Dukkha* combines the prefix *du-*, "bad," and the root *kha*, "hole," as in the axle hole of a cart or a wagon, and so it literally means a badly fitting wheel. That's what suffering is—a badly fitting wheel that jolts and jostles us as we ride along the path of life. Something's off.

The word "dukkha" implies suffering can be transformed—it is itself an invitation to understand and alchemize suffering. After all, what do you do with a badly fitting wheel? You adjust it. You tinker with it to make the ride smoother. It's possible to perceive the causes of suffering at work in ourselves and how we live our lives, and to change them, at least some of the time. We have that power, especially when we practice and work together. Suffering's opposite, *sukha*—meaning happiness, ease, or well-being—is a metaphor for a wheel that fits well and supports a smooth ride. Sukha is in reach for us all. Bumpy roads lead to freedom, connection, and joy.

The Buddha declared, "Suffering is not the true nature of the universe. Suffering is the result of the way we live and of our erroneous understanding of life." As a way out of suffering, he invited us to walk the noble path of mindfulness. The on-ramp is wherever you are right now.

If we pay attention, we see that even though there is pain, there is also joy. There is so much worth living for. The miracle is present in every moment, every breath, every smile, every kind word, every condolence, every high-five and hug. Democracy is built on the strong foundation of hope—hope born from the insight that with presence and dedication, things can change and, in fact, are already changing. There is suffering in life, but there is ease, too. There is injustice in life, but there is justice, too. The lotus grows from the muck. There is mud in life; there is sunlight, too. It might be bumpy going, but there is a path.

GRATITUDE IS *the* FOUNDATIONAL DEMOCRATIC EMOTION

If you're having difficulty experiencing interdependence, try practicing gratitude to connect to yourself, to your fellow beings, and to the life that we share.

Democracy is community; it is based on connection. It does not work unless we are willing to break bread with other people— those we know, and those we don't. Life is an ongoing collaboration. People are already working together in deep and meaningful ways to support our shared life. Before we can get down to the hard work of building community, we must ask ourselves: How can we open our hearts and minds to others? How can we learn to say hello to our fellow beings who we have been conditioned to ignore?

Gratitude, that is how. Gratitude is the foundational democratic emotion. When the world knocks us off balance, gratitude can help us regain our footing, enabling us to return home to common ground with a renewed sense of awe, appreciation, and association.

There are many experiences of gratitude. One of the most profound is the feeling of thanksgiving for life that hits us in moments of mindful presence, as we dwell in the wonder of the present moment and revel in the miracle of simply being alive. The practice of democratic mindfulness extends this existential gratitude to everyone, and everything, that makes this life possible—to our ancestors, to the earth, to our friends and family, to our teachers, even to strangers. In this way, gratitude is a bridge to community leading us out of the desolation of political warfare.

One of the primary causes of suffering is when we divide the inseparable into parts and pit those parts against each other in opposition and competition. Humanity is inseparable—from itself, from the earth, from all living beings. To direct thanksgiving at our fellows is a practice of mending. It is a simple way to care for our suffering by gently reuniting what custom and culture have rendered asunder.

Let us practice living gratefully, so that we might live democratically!

One of my favorite practices of mindful democracy is a gratitude meditation I wrote, inspired by the historical and philosophical study of gratitude I undertook to write *The Art of Gratitude* and by the Plum Village tradition of Thich Nhat Hanh. This meditation is an invitation to see all the ways we are interconnected with other people, other beings, and the earth as a blessing rather than a curse. None of us bear the burden of transforming suffering by ourselves: we get to do it together.

This meditation makes use of a series of *gathas*, short phrases designed to call you back to the wonder of the present moment. On the in-breath, repeat the first line of each stanza in your head; on the out-breath, repeat the second line of each stanza. Then take a few mindful breaths to let the words sink in before moving on to the next stanza.

A quick word about smiling: smiling might seem silly, yet it is a profound mindfulness practice. Smiling is a way to remember that the present moment is a wonderful moment. Smiling promotes a sense of well-being and connection. Smiling is not a way to suppress painful emotions; it is a deep practice to explore for yourself. Look at any statue of the Buddha, and you'll likely see a half-smile of awareness on his lips. The Buddha greeted contingency with a smile. These statues remind us that smiling is a worthy practice—for life is meant to be enjoyed, not endured.

Let's try this practice out, together.

"The Art of Gratitude" Meditation

Breathing in, I know I am breathing in.
Breathing out, I know I am breathing out.

Breathing in, there is only the present moment.
Breathing out, I am grateful for this moment.

Breathing in, I am grateful for the breath.
Breathing out, I smile at the breath.

Breathing in, I am grateful for this body.
Breathing out, I smile at this body.

Breathing in, I am grateful for feelings.
Breathing out, I smile at feelings.

Breathing in, I am grateful for thoughts.
Breathing out, I smile at thoughts.

Breathing in, I am grateful for this life.
Breathing out, I smile at this life.

Breathing in, I am grateful for my ancestors who made my life possible.
Breathing out, I smile at my ancestors.

Breathing in, I am grateful for the people in this life who support me.
Breathing out, I smile at the people in this life who support me.

Breathing in, I am grateful for friends who care for me.
Breathing out, I smile at friends who care for me.

Breathing in, I am grateful for strangers who care for me.
Breathing out, I smile at strangers who care for me.

Breathing in, I am grateful for all I have learned.
Breathing out, I smile at all I have learned.

*Breathing in, I am grateful for the teachers who have taught me what
    I've learned.*
*Breathing out, I smile at the teachers who have taught me what I've
    learned.*

Breathing in, I am grateful for the chance to be here for myself.
Breathing out, I smile at myself.

Breathing in, I am grateful for the chance to be here for others.
Breathing out, I smile at the other people in my life.

Breathing in, I know I am breathing in.
Breathing out, I know I am breathing out.

Close this meditation by pledging to say thank you to the
people in your life who support your practice. If these people say
you're welcome, or if they thank you in return for all you do for
them, hear their message and recognize the profound connection
it represents.

Practicing the art of gratitude is an opening into interdependence that reveals the many blessings of interbeing. Over time,
you may find that, rather than being something we force upon
ourselves, thanksgiving becomes a natural experience that arises
in moments of true presence. We are not Sisyphus, the character
from Greek myth condemned for eternity to roll a boulder up a
hill only to watch it come tumbling back down. I often meditate on
Sisyphus at rest, taking refuge in cooperation and finding safety
in community. We don't have to make peace with an anguishing
fate. We can work together and lend each other a hand. Perhaps
together we can build a ledge that keeps the boulder from thundering back down the hillside.

Practicing mindful democracy involves pausing to notice all the ways we are already caring for each other, and for the life we share, and then taking a moment to feel gratitude for this care. The reality is that we are already helping each other out in a million unseen ways. Every "I" is also a "We." Every life is shared. We don't have to walk the path of life alone. We can go together. And we do.

DEMOCRACY REQUIRES STRONG *and* OPEN HEARTS

Democracy benefits from loving-kindness, or *metta*. This practice helps us be present with the suffering of the world and its many forms of injustice without breaking down or turning against our fellow beings.

Democracy requires us to have big hearts capable of holding great amounts of shared suffering in our awareness without burning out, giving up, or turning against each other. Some of the most important work we do as mindful citizens is to open and strengthen our hearts so we can meet suffering with compassion and injustice with determination.

How do we open our hearts as wide as the world? How do we strengthen our hearts so they can hold the suffering we encounter? How do we expand our hearts to the size of infinity? A mindfulness practice of heart opening that deeply supports this endeavor is called *metta* or "loving-kindness."

Loving-kindness, the feeling cultivated in metta meditation, is very different from romantic love. In the ancient Pali language, the word "metta" has two root meanings. The first is "gentle," in the sense of a gentle spring rain that falls on young plants, nourishing them without discrimination. The second is "friend." With metta practice, we grow our ability to be present for ourselves and others without fail and without demanding anything in return. We become able to support where there is pain and to be happy where there is happiness. Metta is limitless and unbounded love; it is gentle presence and universal friendliness.

Democracy calls for people with big, stout hearts; this is what the practice of metta invites. Why big hearts? I'm reminded of a story I heard told at the Plum Village monastery and practice center in France during a summer retreat: one of the Buddha's students approached him and asked why he emphasized loving-kindness meditation so strongly. The Buddha responded by asking the student to get a cup of salt. Then the Buddha asked the student to pour the salt into a cup of water. "Is it salty?" he asked. The student took a sip and responded, "Yes, very." The Buddha then invited the student to get another cup of salt and pour it into the nearby freshwater lake. "Is it salty?" he asked. The student took a sip and responded, "No, not at all." Suffering is like the salt. If you expand the size of your heart to the size of a lake or an ocean or the entire earth, you can hold suffering without being overwhelmed by it.

To practice metta, or loving-kindness, we offer love without any expectation of it being returned. Metta is not reciprocal or conditional. It does not discriminate between us and them, rich and poor, educated and uneducated, popular or unpopular, worthy and unworthy. To practice metta is to give what I describe in *The Art of Gratitude* as "the rarest and most precious gift": a gift that does not demand a return.

Metta meditation typically begins with a mindfulness practice like mindful breathing or mindful walking to calm the mind and body and come back home to the now. Once we feel more settled and collected, we softly recite several traditional phrases while visualizing those who will receive the loving-kindness we speak. If you'd like to try metta meditation, some typical phrases are:

✳ May I/you/they/we be filled by loving-kindness.

✳ May I/you/they/we be safe from inner and outer dangers.

✳ May I/you/they/we be well in body and mind.

✳ May I/you/they/we be at ease and happy.

Traditionally, we begin with ourselves and first cycle through these phrases using the "I" pronoun. After we have spoken these four phrases, pausing to receive them and to sense into the feeling tone they evoke, we move to the second pronoun listed: "you." Reciting these phrases directed at "you," we picture a beloved person, pet, animal, favorite tree—anything or anyone we would like to direct loving-kindness toward. Next, we insert the "they" pronoun into each phrase and direct our loving-kindness to a wider circle of friends and loved ones. Finally, we gradually include more and more people in our well wishes: the folks in our community and town, people everywhere, animals and all living beings, and the whole earth—in this last round of recitation, the pronoun changes to "we."* In this way, loving-kindness meditation is a practice of opening our hearts further and further to life, beginning with ourselves. Each time we open our hearts like this, we prepare ourselves to practice democracy.

Metta meditation creates a feeling of kinship with all living beings, a sense of unbounded connection that is infinitely spacious and without walls. A big heart is necessary if we are to avoid being dragged into political wars or consumed by bitterness and resentment when we address injustice. Loving-kindness leaps past the divisions created by concepts like "friends" and "enemies" to a renewed sense of interconnection with all who share this miraculous life. To transform resentment, hatred, and fear, it's necessary to match it with a counterforce that is even stronger. That force is metta.

---

* Many versions of this meditation invite practitioners to express metta for people who have caused them difficulty or have hurt them, including someone seen to be an "opponent" or an "enemy." However, teachers including Thich Nhat Hanh recommend practicing metta meditation in this way only once you are well established in directing loving-kindness at yourself and those you are close to—see Thich Nhat Hanh, *Teachings on Love* (Parallax Press, 2007), 37–50.

PART 2

WALK *the* PATH *of* INTER-DEPENDENCE *in* COMMUNITY

To face the challenges of our time demands the full wisdom of humanity in all its magnificent diversity. The big challenges our society must address, the wicked problems that generate the most human suffering, are forms of injustice that cannot be tackled individually. Though what each of us does personally matters—how we live our lives and the choices we make are consequential—big problems require big, societal changes. They require us to work together, as communities, with people different from us—people who look different, who speak

different languages and have very different experiences, values, and ideas. It's time for us to build safe, inclusive, dynamic communities capable of great compassion, places where we learn to practice true democracy by caring for each other and for our shared life.

Let us call these communities "beloved."

DEMOCRACY STARTS *when* WE STOP LIVING *a* LIE

The world's biggest lie is that some people
are naturally more important, and more
deserving of safety, happiness, and well-being,
than other people—we refute this lie.

In our world, people are divided into categories—race, gender, nationality, wealth—and then ranked, creating hierarchies of power and prestige. These categories tend to be binaries; many people are skeptical of those who do not fit neatly into society's boxes or who seek to transgress them. Growing up, we're taught that some people—because of their skin color, or gender, or riches, or where they happened to be born, or the language they speak (or don't speak)—are simply and naturally better than others.

Why do I call this a lie? Because there is nothing inevitable or predestined about who ends up on top of societies. There is no universal law of history that divides people into classes or castes. There is nothing natural or inevitable about how societies are structured, about who is on top and who is on bottom, about who is rich and who is poor, about who is included and who is excluded, about who can speak and who cannot, or who has power and who does not.

Inequality, and all other markers of distinction, are the result of choices that humans have made in the past and that we continue to make today. To think otherwise is to be bamboozled by old, outdated stories about the development of societies invented during the European Enlightenment that still cause great suffering today.

In truth, no one is inherently better than anyone else. Everyone belongs. Everyone is welcome on this planet. Everyone deserves love and respect. Everyone is entitled to feel safe and at peace. Everyone has a right to be happy and free. Everyone should have enough to live, and to thrive, when there is such abundance. Everyone has something to contribute to democracy. With this insight, it becomes possible to stop living a lie and to envision instead a radically different future for humanity.

IT IS IN BELOVED COMMUNITIES THAT WE LEARN *to* PRACTICE DEMOCRACY

In our Beloved Communities,
in practicing caring for each other and
for the life we share, we become a microcosm
of the world we'd like to create.

If we aspire to democracy, we need places where we can learn its skills and practice living the truth of interdependence and all this truth entails. I will call these places "Beloved Communities," using a phrase that inspired two of my personal heroes: Dr. Martin Luther King Jr. and Thich Nhat Hanh.

Before being assassinated on April 4, 1968, at the age of thirty-nine, Dr. King invited a number of his friends to continue his life's work of building the Beloved Community. Thich Nhat Hanh was one of these friends. In the decades since King's death, the aspiration for the Beloved Community has become central to the Plum Village tradition of mindfulness practice. In a letter to his community titled "Climbing Together the Hill of the Century," Thầy wrote:

> *Human rights activist Dr. Martin Luther King yearned to build a beautiful community—a happy community, with solidarity and capacity for activism and engagement. He called such a community "The Beloved Community." Unfortunately, he was assassinated at the age of thirty-nine in Memphis, so he could not realize his beautiful dream. We are more fortunate. We have been able to set up sanghas everywhere, and so wherever we go, we can feel at home. . ... We have continued that aspiration of Dr. Martin Luther King Jr., and every day, our practice is to generate brotherhood and sisterhood, to cultivate joy and the capacity to help people. This is a concrete way to realize and continue that dream.*

What makes a community beloved? The answer is right there in the name, *be-love-ed*. Beloved Communities practice building a shared life based in love, compassion, joy, and peace. Beloved Communities do all they can to help participants awaken the natural ability to care and to understand inside each of us. Beloved Communities are many things: place of refuge, dharma labs to practice mindfulness together, and sources of support. They are also places to practice gratitude and love. The practice of the art of gratitude and loving-kindness meditation is central to the Beloved Community, because these practices prepare our minds and hearts to step outside the political war and to stand instead on common ground. Infusing every word and every deed with thanksgiving and compassion is how participants in Beloved Communities transform a lonely life rooted in competition and separation into a shared life of connection and interbeing. In doing so, we learn to live true democracy.

The Beloved Community Dr. King and Thầy imagined is not an abstraction. It is a loose-knit global community composed of a multitude of smaller, local Beloved Communities committed to practicing peace, compassion, justice, mindfulness, and connection. Each local community addresses injustice as it plays out in their time and place. Each local community determines what they value and what they stand for. Then each community stands up in affirmation for their values in whatever creative, improvisational way they imagine.

Beloved Communities do not set out to wage war on suffering. Hating hate does not work. Waging war on suffering does not work. Making an enemyship out of enemyship does not work. Doing this only adds more hate, suffering, and enemyship to the world. As Dr. King observed in his sermon "Loving Your Enemies," "Hate cannot drive out hate, only love can do that." Beloved Communities practice affirmation, not opposition. Beloved Communities do not divide themselves into hierarchies of better and worse, friends and enemies, or worthy and unworthy. A person is not more important, or more worthy of care, or more deserving of the miracle, because they are wealthy and well-connected and mighty. Everyone is equal. Everyone deserves a chance to answer life's eternal questions in their own words. Everyone, no matter how humble they may seem, has something important to contribute to our shared life.

In our Beloved Communities, we become a microcosm of the world we'd like to create. In our Beloved Communities, we make sure everyone has enough, everyone feels safe and welcome, everyone is valued and treated with respect, and everyone is free to develop their individual talents and gifts. In our Beloved Communities, we practice the art of wise togetherness, for we are awake to interdependence. We are awake to the fact that we are collaborators, not competitors, in the shared miracle of life. We live and work together to make the world a happier and less painful place for all living beings.

In our Beloved Communities, we refute the world's biggest lie that some people don't belong and replace it with truth that we are all worthy of life and liberty. Together, with enough Beloved Communities—and we are talking about thousands and thousands, in all the world's tongues—we practice democracy and gain enough power to mend a fractured world.

= INSIGHT 14 =

THERE IS WISDOM *and* CREATIVITY *in* DIVERSITY

Inclusion matters—
diversity makes us
wiser and more creative.

Mindful citizens make a special effort to make our beloved communities inclusive and diverse. Why is this so important? Because everyone deserves the opportunity to practice self-government. And because wise decisions are made by diverse groups with multiple perspectives and languages who are empowered to deliberate about issues that affect and matter to them.

If everyone in the community looks and talks and thinks the same, our ability to think outside the box (a skill we need more than ever as we face increasing global complexity, climate disruption, and the unraveling of old certainties) is limited. A diverse community brings a wider range of perspectives to the discussion, increasing the likelihood for collective insight. The more diverse we are, the more creative we can be. Together, we see things that alone we miss, and as our collective knowledge and insight grows, so too does our ability to respond skillfully to suffering and injustice. Inclusion makes us wiser; it helps us to better care for each other and for our shared life.

Inclusion is a practice. It involves reaching out to people traditionally excluded from the types of communities we build and actively inviting them in. If they heed the invitation to participate, inclusion becomes a practice of making them feel welcome, making sure they are truly equal, and ensuring their voices are heard.

A basic lesson of propaganda is that if you repeat something often enough and loud enough, many people will believe it, no matter how outlandish it is. Practicing inclusion in our Beloved Communities is a way to counteract an unfortunate reality of the attention economy: the "echo chamber." Online, people tend to gravitate toward others who hold similar views. Social media is the perfect medium for propaganda to take hold. Online communities tend to exclusively share content that agrees with their worldview, forming an echo chamber—different and dissenting voices drop away. Soon communities develop their own vocabulary and memes to signal who belongs, and who doesn't. Belief in the core tenets becomes a point of pride and a marker of identity. Spend some time in an echo chamber, and it will quickly seem like everyone in the world believes what you believe—and those who don't are either crazy or evil. This makes echo chambers particularly susceptible to paranoia and conspiracy theories. Unfortunately, it's hard to make good decisions if we've lost touch with reality, and with our common ground.

We become what we practice. The attention economy teaches us to be good at exclusion. When it comes to the practical everyday need to do something to ease the forms of suffering that affect us all, however, blindly practicing exclusion puts us in grave danger. We cannot care for our shared life if we refuse to talk with people who see the world differently than we do.

Every time we ignore or willfully exclude someone from the conversation, a potential source of genius is lost, and the community grows a little weaker. If everyone looks and sounds the same, the music the ensemble makes will be limited. It will become an echo rather than an original composition.

Let's be clear: to exclude, to speak with prejudice, to persecute, to ostracize, to demean, is to make the community collectively dumber and weaken our ability to address the challenges that drew the community together in the first place. If we're going to transform the injustice in our world—and we must try!—we need all the wisdom and creativity and innovation we can muster. This is why our Beloved Communities must be committed to cultivating a diversity of voices and actively including people who have been excluded.

EVERY I IS ALSO *a* WE

Because every I is also a We,
mindful citizens treat our communities
like an ensemble. Instead of fighting
with our fellows, we learn from each other
as we collaborate on common
projects and challenges.

Part of what is so exhausting about politics today is that we are urged to think of it as a war, and so we are flooded with all the destabilizing, disorienting emotions that accompany war: anger, resentment, hatred, fear. It's draining, especially when all most of us want to do is to live our lives, and to enjoy the miracle of life together. In our Beloved Communities, we set down our arms and commit ourselves to a different practice altogether: being an ensemble.

In French, *ensemble* means "together"; in English, an ensemble is a musical group of people playing or laughing or singing in harmony. But an ensemble is more than that. In jazz, for instance, the players in an ensemble aim to make each other shine. They understand their own brilliance depends upon the ensemble.

Consider the words of one of my favorite musicians, the Grammy and Pulitzer Prize–winning trumpeter Wynton Marsalis, who compared the jazz ensemble to democracy:

> *New Orleans jazz—group improvisation, cooperative ensemble playing—functions exactly like a democracy. Which means each person has the right to play what they want to play, but the responsibility to play something that makes everybody else sound good. . . . the way that these horns relate to the rhythm section, it's like a musical example of how a democracy works.*

The word "ensemble" has special force in the work of the beloved democratic poet Walt Whitman. Writing during the nineteenth century, Whitman repeatedly urges readers to stop, to look closely at our world, to notice everyday miracles, and to observe all the hooks and links that hold us together. Once dubbed the "seer" of democracy, Whitman looks past the unending partisan war toward a more collaborative and empowering future.

He does this, in large part, by making lists and joyfully connecting the dots between entries. Whitman's poetry is famous for listing the people he encounters while sauntering around Brooklyn and Manhattan. Today we're taught to experience other people as separate from us: as competitors in the pursuit of happiness. Whitman challenges this commonsense view by picturing all the people he meets as an ensemble. The beauty of Whitman's lists is that with each line he reiterates the mindfulness foundation of democracy: everyone is equal, everyone has a part to play in the ensemble, and every single person—no matter their gender, or race, or sexual preference, or nationality, or level of wealth—belongs and is worthy of respect and dignity. This is one way to think about democratic "freedom."

In Whitman's poems, the ties that bind people together have nothing to do with blood, tradition, or ancestry. What unites the ensemble is our shared life and our potential to collaborate to make that life happier and less painful.

At the end of one of his many long lists detailing a motley cast of characters, including well-heeled opera singers, duck hunters caked in mud, impoverished painters, bright-eyed tatterdemalions, loud-voiced social reformers, young mothers caring for crying children, and emancipated slaves walking tall with pride, Whitman reflects:

> *And these tend inward to me, and I tend outward to them,*
> *And such as it is to be of these more or less I am,*
> *And of these one and all I weave the song of myself.*

The "song of myself" is the song we sing about who we are, what we value, what we desire, and what matters most to us. When we sing this song, we sing with an individual voice that is our own.

But the air we breathe? The words we use? The melody we hum? These are shared.

Practicing mindfulness together, we experience the power of our own voices in the context of others. The songs we sing can never be just about ourselves. We do not stand apart from the ensemble; we are a part of it. To sing the song of myself is to belt out an autobiographical anthem of ands, a canto of connection, a chant of cooperation, a lullaby of living together, a shanty of shared life and fate. This song is set to the rhythm of the cosmic pulse, to the drum beat of togetherness. It is a song of the one and the many, a song of ensemble, a song of shared responsibility for each other and our shared world.

The song of myself is my song, but I did not write it alone—it is a collaboration. Every *I* is in fact also a *We*. Each of us contains multitudes. When we sing and play and live, we sing and play and live with multitudes.

Practicing mindfulness together in our Beloved Communities, we see it is not just suffering that unites humans—if it were, what a sad and degraded life this would be! The joy, the courage, and the resilience we discover as we face injustice and sorrow also unites us. Practicing together, we discover the potential inside each of us to love and tend in our own way: or, as Whitman so beautifully wrote,

> *I am larger, better than I thought,*
> *I did not know I held so much goodness.*

We are capable of so much more than wounding. We are built for joy and wonder and connection, too. Let us learn from each other, in our Beloved Communities, and be enriched by our differences rather than living to spite them!

WE ARE ONE, *and* WE ARE MANY

The world is both one and many,
and democracy is a complex dance of
individuals and ensembles—interdependence
that demands conformity is not true
interdependence, unity that suppresses
community is not true unity, oneness that
denies diversity is not true oneness.

We are one, *and* we are many.

We are one: we stand on common ground—we are lotus flowers who share the same mud, and the same aspiration, to embrace and enjoy the miracle of life. *We are many*: each of us has our own unique and creative ways of standing tall and growing beautiful lotus flowers from the muck. People are as similar and as varied as the leaves of grass in a field, for we are also interconnected and interdependent.

Based on the insight of interbeing, democracy is a communal practice of embracing the one in the many and the many in the one. Today we are taught to experience democracy as war; we grow used to seeing division, borders, lines, and walls, but not the bridges and roads that run through and across such barriers. No wonder we miss interdependence and overlook the common ground we share.

To say "we are one" is to express true insight, but, as Zen Buddhists caution, the finger that points at the moon is not the moon itself. Our words are not the sunset, though we might miss a beautiful sunset if someone didn't point it out with their words. Our words create a world on top the world, mediating our lives and how we live them. The words we use to gesture to reality are useful. But we experience reality through the lens of the words we use and the stories we know, and if that lens is cracked, or just not the right prescription, our vision will be skewed, and with it, our actions. If we hope to suffer less, we need to see reality more clearly; if we want to see reality more clearly, we need to sit with our words, especially powerful words like "one" and "oneness."

A caution: to be ethical, talk of oneness must not deny or disparage diversity. The interdependence that demands conformity is not true interdependence: it is tyranny. In many traditions, talk of oneness is an excuse to ignore what makes us unique. We must take care that invocations of oneness do not become lazy affirmations that all people are basically the same. We must also take care that talk of oneness does not become a demand that we must be all the same. True democracy does not demand conformity. Disagreement is healthy, as long as it comes from a place of mindfulness. Our distinctions are not delusions. The world is both one and many. We live in a pluralistic universe. There are and should be many ways to build a good life.

It's just that underneath our differences, we are bound. We walk a common path. We share a common world. We live a common life. We will experience a common fate.

Practicing mindfulness in our Beloved Communities, we honor oneness, though we do not strive to speak with one voice. We also honor diversity, remembering always that what connects us is stronger than what divides. The communities we build are experiments of seeing the one in the many and the many in the one; they will be as varied as the people who gather and as united as the joy and suffering we share.

ENEMYSHIP WRECKS DEMOCRACY *by* TRANSFORMING IT *into* WAR

The moment an enemy is named,
a state of war exists. Enemyship is to
be avoided because it transforms
democracy into a war, and the
surest way to destroy democracy
is to treat it like battle.

Many human communities are based on enemyship, the rhetoric of "us versus them." Such rhetoric is powerful, but it splits people right down the middle and encourages us to ignore all that we share. "You are either with us or against us," the purveyor of enemyship says—in a voice I imagine sounds like John Wayne's rough-hewn chapparal drawl, all while one hand rests on the trigger of a gun even while the other shakes your hand. If we look at the world through divided eyes, we cannot see things clearly, and we miss the common ground on which we stand. I worry that many people, habituated to uniting in opposition to shared enemies, have begun to think this is the only way people can come together.

Enemyship is ancient—read Homer's *Iliad* or the epic Indian poem *The Mahabharata*, and you'll see enemyship canonized as the wisdom of the gods. People have practiced enemyship for millennia, so you might think it is somehow innate to being human. My first book is called *Enemyship*, and the most surprising thing I discovered while writing that book is that enemyship does not persist because it's natural—there is no evolutionary biology wiring that causes human beings to see the world as a conflict between friends and enemies. If there were, we humans would have destroyed ourselves long ago! Enemyship persists because it is politically useful for perpetuating the world's biggest lie, especially for those at the top of the social hierarchy who want to protect their place there by keeping the people below them in their place, too.

The key difference between a Beloved Community and a community based in enemyship is that enemyship stands *against* something—historically, it is often against another group of people—while democracy grounded in a mindful insight into interdependence stands *for* something—namely, for the commitment to care for our shared life and to meet suffering together.

People practicing democracy are free to speak up and to speak out about issues that directly affect them. In contrast, enemyship seeks to curtail disagreement and dissent. Enemyship demands unity in opposition to an enemy—its mantras are "us against them," and "you're either with us or against us." Though the unity enemyship demands is rarely achieved, it provides perfect cover for authorities to silence protestors and smear dissenters as traitors in league with the enemy. Enemyship is a form of what I call "toxic oneness." It might feel like strength to participate in the battle, but in fact war is a form of social control that transforms us into reactive, fractured beings.

Enemyship is repression, for it seeks to rob us of the present moment by flooding this moment with stress, anxiety, and fear. A mantra of enemyship is *there is no time*. There is no time to question the status quo, no time to call out the injustices you see, no time to build communities committed to change. There is no time to reflect or to ask, "Are you sure?"—the barbarians are already at the gates! Grab your arms! Rage! Fight! Kill! In moments of enemyship, there is no time to ask questions and raise objections, there is no time to slow down and look deeply, no time to speak lovingly and listen mindfully, so we rush onward to our doom while the bombs (rhetorical and otherwise) fall around us.

Enemyship is ancient, and it is omnipresent. I suspect it is a temptation built into the very nature of language itself. The seeds of enemyship have been planted in our consciousness, and like a weed that cannot be killed, they are always prepared to sprout. Even the healthiest, most mindful democracies need to remain vigilant for the persistent human habit to turn communities into enemyships during crisis.

Though enemyship cannot be eliminated completely, Beloved Community is a tangible alternative. With mindfulness practice, we can notice the seeds of enemyship inside our consciousness and choose not to water them. We can water seeds of love, compassion, and understanding instead. And as our Beloved Communities act, we must be careful not to nourish enemyships with our words—for the moment that we do, our community is no longer so beloved.

Enemyship says there is no time, but if we practice mindfulness, there is always time. Enemyship says we live at high noon, on the precipice of violence, but if we practice mindfulness, we live each moment of the day. Enemyship transforms democracy into a war—the minute an "enemy" exists, war exists, too—but if we practice mindfulness, we can build strong and healthy communities based on something other than enemyship: on caring for each other, and our shared life.

NO PERSON IS "EVIL," *only* "MISTAKEN"

Democracy requires people to collaborate,
and whenever people work together,
conflicts arise. When we disagree,
it's skillful to treat others as
"mistaken" rather than "evil."

Democracy depends upon using words wisely. With wise words, it's possible to live and work together, even in disagreement. With the right words, we can pursue the noble work of transforming suffering into happiness together and resolve conflicts peacefully when they arise (and they always do).

Scrolling through a social media feed is like hearing the drums of battle calling us to war. Today, politicians routinely describe their opponents as "enemies," disparaging them as "evil," "monsters," "demons," and "garbage." To call someone "evil," a "monster," or a "demon" damages democracy, for it undermines cooperation and promotes distrust between people who must learn to live, work, and thrive together. Some may think evil people can only be defeated, through violence if necessary. If people "on the other side" are irredeemable devils, the potential for civic cooperation is undercut—what's the point of trying to understand, and to work with, someone who is "evil"? If the person you disagree with were "evil," it would make no sense to talk to them or try to understand them. You cannot cooperate with an "evil" person. All you can do is try to destroy them.

There is a profound optimism at the heart of most Buddhist traditions, rooted in the foundational belief that everyone is blessed with the capacity to practice mindfulness—to slow down, to find their footing, to see things clearly, and to act with deliberation and compassion. To practice mindfulness is to shift from a reactive to a more deliberate and considered way of living. By mindfully paying attention to habitual reactions and choosing to cultivate habits of compassion, understanding, and peacefulness, everyone is capable of feeling more stable and connected.

A Zen lesson seems particularly apt in this moment of enemyship: treat people you disagree with as mistaken rather than evil.

To illustrate this, in his book *Old Path White Clouds: Walking in the Footsteps of the Buddha,* Thich Nhat Hanh tells the story of Angulimala, a notorious murderer who lived during the Buddha's time. The story goes like this: upon entering the town of Shravasti one morning, the Buddha finds the streets empty, the doors locked, and the windows closed. Angulimala is in town! Though the residents beg him to hide, the Buddha fearlessly continues his walk. Angulimala spots him and shouts for him to stop, but the Buddha does not stop. "I told you to stop, monk. Why don't you stop?" Angulimala demands. The Buddha responds, "I stopped a long time ago. It is you who have not stopped."

This puzzles Angulimala. He asks for an explanation. The Buddha replies, "Angulimala, I stopped committing acts that cause suffering to other living beings a long time ago. I have learned to protect life—the lives of all beings, not just humans. Angulimala, all living beings want to live. All fear death. We must nurture a heart of compassion and protect the lives of all beings."

Angulimala is struck by how the Buddha speaks to him: not as a monster, but with patience and a genuine desire to help him find peace. The Buddha insists that Angulimala, too, can change, if he commits to developing his capacity for mindfulness—and he offers Angulimala a model for how, and why, to change. The two men continue talking, and soon Angulimala reveals his deepest fear: he wants to change his ways—he is deeply unhappy—but he is afraid society will never forgive him for what he has done, and this fear prevents him from stopping long enough to try to reform. The Buddha promises his community will protect Angulimala if he commits to living mindfully, without violence, in harmony with others—and if he agrees to make amends through compassionate acts toward the families and communities he wronged.

Angulimala commits, and eventually he gets a new name: Ahimsaka, the "nonviolent one."

At times, humans commit acts worthy of being deemed "evil." This is not because they are demons; it is because they act out of greed and ignorance and fear. Greed can be overcome; ignorance can be enlightened; fear can be tamed. The parable of Angulimala reflects a worldview that no person is truly "evil," no one an irredeemable monster. Everyone can learn to practice mindfulness. True democracy adopts this worldview. There is always a path out of darkness. Even in the midst of suffering, the conditions for transformation are present.

In June 2024, I participated in a two-week retreat on "Engaged Buddhism" at the Plum Village monastery in France. There I heard a very different vocabulary than that of many politicians—people on the other side of a disagreement were not "evil," they were "mistaken," "ill-informed," "heedless," "unskilled," "unaware" or "unmindful."

Making this small rhetorical change is not easy, especially in times of fear and uncertainty. However, even this slight shift creates a profound practical difference in the moral argument of politics. If someone is mistaken, it makes sense to talk with them, to attempt to understand them, and then, if the situation is right, to try to persuade them to see things differently.

The next time you are in a disagreement and you feel the urge to label someone as "evil" or "vicious" or a "monster," pause. Take three mindful breaths. Feel the earth under your feet. Be where you are standing. Try picturing the person or people you disagree with as mistaken or unmindful. Recognize that their perspective, so opposed to yours, is not the sum total of who they are—there are parts of them you will never know, deep longings and fears and joys born from an autobiography both like and unlike yours. Recognize that though you disagree on this point, they are, like you, a being that fears death, and shuns sadness, and wants to be happy and at peace, a being capable of mindfulness, a being whose life, like yours, is a miracle. Notice if your mindset shifts. And then make a choice about how you want to respond—for that is the beauty of mindfulness practice: it helps you recover your agency as a human being. Notice if this makes it any easier to work together.

Let this be a quiet practice: to speak in ways that leave room for recognition, for repair. This is how democracy endures—not through erasing conflict, but through refusing to harden our hearts against those who share our planet.

PART 3

PRACTICE DEMOCRACY *with* HANDS *and* HEART

✳ ✳ ✳ ✳ ✳

Once we have built Beloved Communities, it is time to face the suffering of the world and to do what we can to alleviate it. Action is not detached from our mindfulness practice; often, it is a deep sense of interdependence that gives us the capacity and the inspiration to turn toward the suffering of others. The actions we take together to address harm aim to wake people up to the reality of injustice, to show how injustice affects us all, and then to convince others not to participate in its perpetuation. All the while, we provide an alternative way of living together that prioritizes love, compassion, joy, and peace.

THERE IS NO WAY *to* DEMOCRACY, DEMOCRACY IS THE WAY

Democratic power is not physical power:
it is not domination; democratic power is
spiritual power: it is the power we collectively
generate from building safe, inclusive,
and vibrant communities in which we care
for each other and for our shared life.
We refuse to participate in the creation
of hell to achieve heaven.

Thich Nhat Hanh used to say, "There is no way to peace, peace is the way." The same is true for democracy. The way we move, the way we speak, the way we show up for one another—these are not rehearsals for democracy; they are democracy. You can't use undemocratic or anti-democratic means to achieve democracy. You can't build democratic communities with violence or enemy-ship. Only democracy can build democracy. This is the reason I like to tell my students, "There is no way to democracy, democracy is the way."

Democracy is a practice, a noun we must also understand as a verb, a form of collective action. Our English word "democracy" is derived from the Ancient Greek *demokratīa*, a combination of the words *krātos*, "power" or "rule," and *dēmos*, "the community" or "the people." "Democracy," then, literally means "the power of the community to govern itself." Power is a slippery word, of course, capable of papering over all manner of sin. When it comes to "power," I find Mahatma Gandhi's distinction between "physical power" (the power that comes from domination, exclusion, and repression) and "spiritual power" (the power that arises from respect, inclusion, and collaboration) helpful. Physical power is the power of armies. Spiritual power is the power of democratic communities committed to caring for each other and for the life we share.

Democratic power is not physical power: it is not domination. That's what we've gotten so terribly wrong in thinking democracy is a fight or a battle or a war we must win by dominating and defeating our enemies. War is division. War splinters the world into friends and enemies. War dehumanizes. War degrades. War destroys. In stark contrast, true democracy is a practice of affirmation. The strategy of waging war for democracy is counter-productive, because democratic power is spiritual power: it is the power we collectively generate from building safe, inclusive, and vibrant communities in which we care for each other and for our shared life. You can't create spiritual power with physical power. You can't build an arsenal of democracy; you can't wage a war for democracy (or for peace). Democratic power is the power of collaboration, not combat.

Democracy starts from what we share. Democracy builds connections and bridges. Democracy welcomes and includes. Democracy is not a war. The people we disagree with are not enemies, they are people, just like us, who suffer, just like us, and who have hopes and dreams and fears, just like us. We must meet them on common ground.

People who go to war are soldiers. People who practice democracy are citizens. Mindful citizens take responsibility for the world together. We do not commit violence. We treat ourselves and others with respect and dignity. We are aware that politics is a moral argument and that the most effective arguments start from what we hold in common, not what divides us. We remember that life is a miracle we share and that we are interconnected even when we disagree. With every word and every deed, we declare our interdependence.

Mindful citizens embody the world we seek to create in our thoughts, in our words, and in our actions. When we act, we do our best to ensure we do not add to the suffering of the world. We ask ourselves, "Are you sure?" and we double- and triple-check that our words and deeds do not affirm the divisions or oppositions that transform life into a war. We model a way of caring for our shared life. We refuse to participate in the creation of hell to achieve heaven. We remember the foundational insight of mindfulness practice: the present moment is the only moment. And we remember that each moment is a wonderful moment, even when painful, because the conditions for the transformation of that pain into care or even joy are also present.

We have hands and feet. We have a voice. We have each other. We are not stuck. We have agency. We can act. In every moment we choose mutual care over conquest, we are not preparing the ground for democracy—we are standing on it.

MINDFUL CITIZENS CARE: WE DO NOT ACQUIESCE *to* INJUSTICE *or* BOW *to* THE STATUS QUO

Because the only thing injustice
needs to persist is a bored shrug
of the shoulders and a casual "whatever,"
we refuse to acquiesce.

Injustice does not demand a big thumbs up and an active endorsement to persist. All it needs is a bored shrug of the shoulders and a casual "whatever." All it needs is acquiescence. "The broadest and most prevalent error requires the most disinterested virtue to sustain it," Henry David Thoreau wrote—with a wink, for it's not "virtue" to remain disinterested when confronted with injustice.

One of the most common misperceptions of mindfulness is that it means taking comfort in the world just as it is. But we do not practice mindfulness to grow cold or apathetic, to spiritually bypass the challenges of our shared life or to give up on addressing harm. Right mindfulness is not a sedative. It is a deep seeing— an unflinching gaze that pierces through the noise and numbing of daily life. Mindfulness helps us get beneath all the distractions and see to the heart of things. In the stillness it brings, mindfulness shows us what is true and calls us to respond with the care that is our true nature. This is not a turning away, but a turning toward. It is a devotion to clarity and compassion in equal measure. The insights of our mindfulness practice reveal the world to us, and they show us how to transform our individual and shared realities. They call us to bring our full presence into the communal work of democracy, into collective action rooted in something sturdier than outrage or fear, and we set about doing exactly that.

Some mindfulness teachers argue that any emphasis on social justice is a corruption of the practice. Mindfulness is about accepting reality, they say, and finding our peace within it. In response, I look to Thich Nhat Hanh's practice of "Engaged Buddhism." Born in 1926 in central Vietnam, Thầy entered Từ Hiếu monastery in Huế at the age of sixteen. As a young Buddhist monk living in a nation confronted by colonialism, conflict, and war, he developed the doctrine of "Engaged Buddhism," premised on the belief that working to relieve suffering in the world is enlightenment. As I have endorsed in these pages, Thầy describes the fruit of mindfulness practice as the insight into interdependence, or what he called "interbeing." This insight naturally turns us toward others, toward community, and toward communal effort to reduce the suffering of the world.

During the mid-1960s amid the Vietnam War (called the "American War" in Vietnam), Thầy founded the School of Youth for Social Services to practice Engaged Buddhism and help those affected by the bombs raining down on their homes. At this time, he also founded the Order of Interbeing, an international order of lay peace activists (who are not monks or nuns) committed to embodying the *bodhisattva* ideal—people like myself who devote their lives to alleviating the suffering of the world. During the war, Thầy refused to take a side; he stood for peace and against "intolerance, hatred, and discrimination. These are real enemies of man—not man himself." While battle raged, Thầy and his students risked their lives to provide food, housing, medical care, and sanctuary to the wounded and displaced. For his efforts, Thầy's friend Dr. Martin Luther King Jr. nominated him for the Nobel Peace Prize in 1967. No award was given that year, however, perhaps to protest King's choice to make his nomination letter public. (Nominations were typically private, but King used his to call out the injustice of the Vietnam War.)

Thầy had the courage to stand against war, enemyship, and totalitarianism. Hundreds of thousands of people have decided to live a more ethical life by honoring the "five mindfulness trainings" Thầy and his community wrote: Reverence for Life; True Happiness; True Love; Loving Speech and Deep Listening; and Nourishment and Healing. Thầy's courage earned him a thirty-nine-year exile from his homeland. During his years abroad, he and his students founded the Plum Village monastery in southern France in 1982 (and, in subsequent years, many other Zen monasteries around the world, including three US centers: Blue Cliff in New York, Deer Park in California, and Magnolia Grove in Mississippi). Today, these monasteries serve as practice centers and refuges for daring people who stand up for peace and need a safe place to regroup and recharge.

Thầy writes, "with the insight of interbeing—that we are inherently interconnected with all other beings—we know that when other people suffer less, we suffer less. And when we suffer less, other people suffer less." Though he does not say so explicitly, this insight turns us toward democracy. Worldly action to alleviate suffering is not a distraction from the practice; it is the blossoming of the lotus. The perspective that caring about others is an artificial emphasis on social justice reveals a mindfulness that has yet to fully penetrate the heart.

Life can change. But it cannot change unless we have the courage to face it, to look deeply at it, and to understand it, together. Once we have done this, it's time to act, together. Mindfulness is the courage to face the present moment, to see things clearly, and to accept that yes, indeed, this is happening. Think of all the capacity that is freed up when our energy isn't going to hiding from, or resisting, the reality of what is really happening! It's time to practice democracy. Mindful citizens do not acquiesce.

DEMOCRACY IS ABOUT WINNING HEARTS, NOT WARS

True democracy is nonviolent.
Democracy is not a war between enemies;
it is an argument between equals,
and so when we speak and act, our aim
is persuasion, not domination.

Politics is an argument, which is very different from a war. In a war, the goal is to win at any cost. This includes forcing another person to do what we want them to do. Though we might "win" a war through physical or verbal domination, we do not win the minds and hearts of those we bully (and in fact, we likely stoke rebellion). In an argument, the goal is not to dominate, but to win over the hearts and minds of those who stand opposed. An argument preserves the freedom of all parties even as it seeks to shape the choices an "opponent" makes, bringing them around to our way of seeing and doing things.

Politics is a *moral* argument because it concerns the most vital of matters: what is true, good, right, and just. To participate in politics as a citizen is to take a moral stand about how we should live our lives. Those who stand together on the common ground of interbeing and who remember the miracle of life have spiritual power—Gandhi called it "satyagraha," or "truth force"—the steadfast determination to stand against lies, deception, and injustice. This is why democracy cannot be a war, why instead it must be committed to peace. Democracy loses its moral authority to inspire change the moment it becomes a war or a fight.

It's all too common for the people in charge of nations and communities to abandon argument and adopt violence. Such leaders believe in what I call "the rule of bullies." For them, might makes right, and violence is perfectly acceptable when it serves their interests. Bullies want to redefine morality as a struggle for self-preservation and the survival of the fittest, because that is their language and their worldview. When bullies rule, they seek to reduce discourse to the level of threats and lies. Bullies practice physical power, aka domination, and their weapon is fear. Bullies want others to respond to their aggression with violence:

when they do, force is further legitimized as the way things get done.

The rule of bullies is a historical constant. There are people who deny the truth of interbeing and who wish to dominate their fellow beings in every time and place. Bullies seem powerful, and it's true that they are destructive. However, history shows the rule of bullies is fragile. When people resist bullies democratically, mindfully, and nonviolently, the rule of tyranny more often than not will end. Indeed, scholars studying political change have shown, definitively, that large-scale nonviolent democratic civil disobedience during the twentieth and twenty-first centuries was more effective than violent resistance at producing social change.

Democracy gains its moral authority from a deep commitment to deliberation, argument, and the free exchange of ideas between equals. When it is time to act together as a community to draw attention to injustice and to persuade people to stop participating in it, we must be committed to doing so without violence or division.

To illuminate injustice and encourage people to see the world differently, mindful citizens can engage in nonviolent speech and action as a Beloved Community. Gandhi pioneered the art of nonviolent resistance to the rule of bullies on a large scale in India in the early 1900s. Proponents of civil rights in the United States understood that politics is a moral argument. Beginning in the 1920s and 1930s, many Black American civil rights activists, including one of my heroes, the Reverend James Lawson, traveled to India to learn from Gandhi and his students how they could adopt these techniques to the struggle for racial equality in the United States. They aimed to persuade their fellow citizens that injustice was real, and that it affected us all.

In his essay "Pilgrimage to Nonviolence," Dr. Martin Luther King Jr., reflected, "Nobody can win a war. The choice today is no longer between violence and nonviolence. It is either nonviolence or nonexistence." Protestors during the early years of the Civil Rights Movement made a commitment to nonviolence, including not to react to injustice with hatred or violence. The early successes of the Civil Rights Movement against racial segregation and oppression in the late 1950s and early 1960s were due, in large measure, to how successful brilliant men and women were in adapting nonviolence to the American scene. "As the days unfolded," Dr. King wrote, "the inspiration of Mahatma Gandhi began to exert its influence. . . . Nonviolent resistance had emerged as the technique of the movement, while love stood as the regulating ideal."

What makes democracy—rooted in mindful presence, embodied insight into interdependence, and nonviolent, loving action—effective in the face of deception, lies, and injustice? Nonviolence is effective because it highlights injustice and its effects without physically hurting those who perpetuate the injustice (or who allow it to continue). By choosing nonviolence, the Beloved Community proves it is not an enemy. It wants to hurt no one. It refuses to react to life's challenges with enemyship. What it wants is healing, connection, and transformation. Nonviolence is effective because it invites people into the Beloved Community, rather than pushing them away with demands for violent confrontation. True democracy seeks to awaken the deep goodness present even in oppressors.

Mindful citizens are careful to ensure the moral argument of politics does not become a war or a street fight that we falsely believe can be solved with violence. The goal of true democracy is not to dominate and defeat the bullies. The goal is to change the oppressors' minds by speaking to their hearts. Democracy is a form of "moral jujitsu" that throws attackers off-balance. It aims to inspire one's "opponents"—and society at large—to reflect on injustice and build spiritual power, not physical power.

DELIBERATION IS *the* CORNERSTONE *of* DEMOCRACY

When practicing democracy,

deliberation precedes action.

Most of us never learned how to deliberate.

That's okay. We can learn now.

What do people committed to democracy actually do?

We build Beloved Communities.

We care for each other.

We think deeply together.

We practice mindful deliberation.

We make wise decisions.

And then we act, skillfully, to relieve the suffering of the world.

Deliberation is the practice of engaging in thoughtful discussion to make informed decisions, and as such it is one of humanity's greatest inventions. Deliberation is a way to practice mindfulness together. Mindful deliberation is how we make the best decisions we can under the present circumstances, with the information we have at hand. When we deliberate in shared mindfulness, we collectively pause before responding to life's challenges. We consider, to the best of our shared knowledge and insight, what is really going on, what is causing it, what we should do about it. To deliberate mindfully is to tap into the immense intelligence that exists whenever a group of people gathers in community.

There is something empowering about being asked to deliberate and to participate in making decisions that affect us, especially when we are constantly confronted with conversations that don't matter at all. It's true that it's impossible to control the future. Nevertheless, a decision reached by deliberation, and that has the collective buy-in of the community, is more likely to be wise than the decision of a tyrant acting by whim and fiat.

Deliberation involves asking questions, raising thoughtful objections, imagining counterexamples and counterfactuals, considering how a decision might affect multiple stakeholders, and sometimes simply asking, "What if...?" or "Did you...?" or "Did you notice ...?" Deliberation is a creative process. No one can predict how a deliberation will play out once it begins. That's part of the fun. Deliberation is an act of improvisation and creativity on the part of a democratic ensemble that trusts each other to play their parts and to have each other's backs.

Deliberation is education. Practicing deliberation, we learn from each other, and the democratic ensemble sings with new possibility. Entirely new futures and worlds we had never even dared to consider suddenly seem possible. Deliberation is an art of transcendence. When we deliberate, we quickly see that the conditions to address and transform injustice are already present. When people deliberate, the status quo trembles.

Wise decisions are made mindfully, together. Wise decisions recognize that change begins with the present moment and how we choose to meet it, together. To teach my college students how to deliberate, I share what I call "The Five Agreements of Mindful Deliberation." These five deliberative agreements highlight the fact that, in a wise community, how we make a decision matters as much as the decision itself. When we deliberate, we go from being a random group of people who happen to be in the same place at the same time to becoming a community. It's by deliberating that we learn just how interconnected we are. It's by deliberating that members of a community come to feel beloved to each other. The five agreements are a guide to practicing deliberation with your community.

THE FIVE AGREEMENTS OF MINDFUL DELIBERATION

"We are all in this together." This is a deliberation, not a debate, and the outcome affects us all. We win, or lose, together. It's vital to identify all the stakeholders (including non-humans) who will be affected by our decision and to determine what the impact will be, for them as well as for those of us in the room.

"Speak up! And listen up!" Everyone is invited to talk— we need your perspective, and your wisdom—but no one should dominate the conversation. Mindful listening is as important as talking. Everyone is equal in the moment of address. Everyone participating is of equal worth. Make space for those who seem hesitant to speak up and for those who have been excluded in the past.

"Stay on Topic." Deliberation does not work if some people talk about one thing while others talk about something else. A deliberating community must constantly remember to bring its collective attention back to the topic under consideration, and to the present moment. In deliberation, we identify the challenge or issue that brings us together today as clearly as possible and stick to it, letting old ghosts, resentments, tangents, and red herrings lie.

"Practice the five questions." Deliberation is not an academic exercise. It is a practice with real-world consequences. When you speak up, you must give reasons for your beliefs, support those reasons with the best, most credible evidence you can muster, and make arguments based on logic and evidence. To say, "This is my truth," without any other support, or to say,

"I feel this deeply in my heart, so it must be true," is not good enough in a deliberation—the well-being of the community is at stake. That's why we practice the five questions: they transform opinions into arguments, and arguments into wisdom:

* What are the pros of this position?

* What are the cons?

* What are the unknowns and the questions we are not equipped to answer at this point?

* What quality evidence do we have to support or oppose this position/policy (while remembering a personal opinion or a gut feeling by itself is not quality evidence)?

* And, finally, what will we do if we are wrong?

"It's okay to change your mind." As you listen and learn, it's okay to change your mind. This is not "flip-flopping." It's education, and education is always good. It is a stepping stone to wisdom, connection, and transformation.

These agreements are an invitation to remember that how you deliberate is just as important as any decision you make. Make deliberation a practice of community mindfulness—it is how we learn to live, and work, and thrive, together.

If you explore mindful deliberation in your community (and I very much hope you do), you might begin your deliberation by practicing mindful breathing to help everyone arrive together in the present moment. Try reading through the five agreements together. Set a collective intention to remember life is a miracle, and to thank each other for the support that is offered. If your deliberation leads you to concrete, practical things you can do to alleviate shared suffering in the world, and to affirm shared joys, that's great. But remember, deliberation takes time. It might take several gatherings to reach a resolution, if you reach one at all. Deliberation happens in our Beloved Communities; it is also how these communities are built and made beloved.

CHANGING YOUR MIND IS NOT WEAKNESS; IT IS THE WORK *of a* BRAVE SOUL

Disagreement is healthy—
it is democracy in motion. We manage
disagreement with deliberation.
The purpose of deliberation is not for one
person or group of people to win, which tends
to be the goal of a debate. The purpose
is to make the best possible decision we can
under the present circumstances with the
information we have. To be open to learning
from others is to be courageous.

Anytime humans gather, disagreement is bound to happen. When people disagree, it is not a mark that we are being unmindful, or disrespectful. Disagreement is an opportunity to practice mindfulness and apply the civic skills we learn from building beloved communities. Disagreement is the bumpy road that leads us to a happier, freer, more supportive and caring future, together.

We live in a culture that loves fighting. The paradox is that most people are terrified of disagreement. People will go to great lengths to avoid it, and no one wants to be told they are "wrong" or misinformed. However, disagreement is not a flaw in the fabric of shared life. It is shared life. It's by disagreeing that we further clarify what the issues are important, and how we determine the strength or weakness of the decisions we might make. To awaken democracy, we must learn to disagree with each other without transforming friction into fracas, or controversy into combat.

We manage disagreement with deliberation. Deliberation is not a performance. The point is not to be the smartest person in the room. Or to constantly poke holes in the arguments of others. Or to say catchy, noteworthy, over-the-top things that will ensure videos of you speaking go viral on social media (though this seems to be the motivation of many politicians and influencers, who appear to be trying their hardest to be the most outrageous, or the most hateful, or the angriest person). Think of deliberation this way: everyone who participates wins or loses together, as a community, because the decisions we make affect us all, as a community. Life is a miracle we share, and your actions affect me just as surely as my actions affect you.

People often remain quiet—even when they have something to say—because they are afraid others will disagree with them. But it's so essential that you speak up! You, too, have something important to contribute to the deliberation, even if it's a simple question. Sometimes a wise question can change everything. Can you mentally reframe disagreement, seeing it not as a danger to your ego but as an opportunity to learn? Can you let go of the old, tired "democracy-as-war" metaphor? Can you see the possibility of being "wrong" as an opportunity for personal insight, and as a moment that can lead the community to greater wisdom?

When deliberating, personal concerns of winning or losing are, at best, irrelevant. Whether or not you, your side, your team, or your party "wins" is not the point. If triumph is your motive, it will lead everyone off the path toward wise and skillful action. At worst, the need to "win" is an invitation to make bad decisions that put individual ego ahead of the common good.

As you deliberate, remember to practice mindfulness. Remember to be kind to yourself. Remember that, when deliberating, it's okay to know, it's okay not to know, and it's okay to admit when you don't know. It's okay to breathe into tension in your gut, or tightness in your chest. Give yourself permission to ask questions when you have questions, and to seek clarity when things are unclear. Remember none of us see the world as gods supposedly do, with complete clarity, objectivity, and omniscience. Remember everyone is capable of learning and transformation, including yourself. Remember it's okay to disagree, okay to be wrong, and okay to change your mind. The fruit of every type of mindful practice, including mindful deliberation, is clarity.

If someone presents information during a deliberation that opposes what you believe, take a moment to pause and to notice any resistance that arises in you. Practicing mindfulness helps us to be less reactive when we identify too closely with our views and feel personally attacked during deliberations. Ask yourself, do

you disagree because the point is untrue, or because you're cling-
ing to your own position, refusing to let it go? Many politicians
today stress ideological purity above all else: every party has its
set of doctrines, and you must stick to them or lose your credibil-
ity and your voice. This is a recipe for battle, not deliberation, for
destruction, not democracy.

Rarely does deliberation present us with a zero-sum, "either/
or," "A or B" choice. Life is not that simple. All enemyships are
false. Often there are a range of possible decisions we can make,
and the actions we choose are limited only by our creativity and
our ethics. There are almost always more than two sides to any
disagreement. Changing your mind during conversation is not
flip-flopping. Making the wisest decision we can under the present circumstances requires us to be open to listening and learning
from our fellows.

To learn from one's errors and to change one's mind, as an
individual and a member of a community, is not shameful or cow-
ardly. So long as you are moved by good reasons, there is no shame
in advocating one position, only to end the deliberation standing on different (though still common) ground. Learning is never
shameful, and it is the farthest thing from cowardice. To learn
and grow takes tremendous courage—and we are courageous.

THE TRUE POWER *of* WORDS IS MENDING

Mindful citizens use words wisely,
with care, in order to mend,
not to fracture.

When we were children, we used to say: "Sticks and stones may break my bones, but words will never hurt me." What a strange refrain! A foundational insight of mindful democracy is that words can wound. Deeply. They can also mend. Completely. Speech is a practice, as is listening. Our relationships are built and sustained by good communication. As we learn to care for each other and for the life we share, one form this care takes is becoming more mindful about the words we speak and how they land.

The attention economy of social media has wrecked the way many people communicate. Here I'm not talking about indecipherable abbreviations or replacing words with inscrutable emojis. I'm talking about how online engagements have caused us to forget our shared humanity.

Social media interactions tend to be with anonymous avatars. They might be people, they might be bots, it's hard to know. Either way, in these interactions we face no real-life repercussions or consequences for what we say. Sadly, there is a real incentive to be controversial, divisive, and even hateful online, for that is the type of content most algorithms promote. Words can hurt. But online, when you post something horrible, or pop into a chat or the comments on a post to say something hateful, you never have to reckon with the hurt it causes to real people. You don't have to see another person's facial expression or experience their tears.

Democracy asks us to recognize that our words have consequences on real people—people who suffer, just like us, and people who want to be happy, just like us. Online, everything is so ephemeral that care with words is not required. Just wait an hour, and people will forget what you said. In person, in the present moment, care is needed. The smiles and the tears are real.

The twin mindfulness practices of *loving speech* and *mindful listening* are central to democracy. In Beloved Community, we practice the art of speaking and listening with care—so when it's time to act in the world, and to engage in the moral argument of politics, we will have good habits. Loving speech comes from the heart and a deep connection with other people. Its goal is understanding. If it is persuasive, this persuasion happens not through trickery or deception—loving speech moves others in the way of the sun shining on a tender plant in spring. Mindful listening involves hearing another person's words with loving-kindness, patience, and compassion. Both practices recognize that other people are not evil, nor are they enemies. We speak, and listen, while standing on common ground.

To develop these practices, I offer you a list of questions. Though it's certainly not practical to ask yourself each of these questions every time you communicate with others, becoming familiar with them now will help you to develop a strong practice of loving speech and mindful listening.

Rather than rushing through to get to the end, I invite you to take time to consider and reflect on each question. Read each question, take a deep breath or two to allow it to sink in, and then sit with it for a few moments before moving on to the next one. Let the consideration of these questions become a practice of mindfulness. Let these questions teach you something about yourself and your communication style. Let them help you become a more loving communicator and a more loving member of your community. Developing the habits of mindful listening and loving speech now, in moments of capacity, will support your ability to turn to them in times of stress. So don't wait to get started. Now is the perfect moment.

WHEN SPEAKING, ASK YOURSELF:

* Are my words necessary?

* Do I talk from the heart, with love?

* Do I speak thoughtfully, with deliberation?

* Do I talk with a determination to relieve suffering rather than adding to it?

* Do I speak with full understanding that my words impact others?

* Do I talk with awareness that my words can help, and also harm?

* Do I speak honestly?

* Do I hold my tongue when my words will wound?

* Do I share my suffering in a way that can be held by others?

* When I am hurting, do I share my hurt in a way that does not hurt others, and my trauma in a way that does not re-traumatize others?

* Do I stand firm against lies, deceptions, paranoia, propaganda, and conspiracy theories?

* Do I refuse to reiterate the world's biggest lie, that some people are naturally better than others and therefore more deserving of security, peace, and happiness?

* Do I remember that I address real people, with real hopes and dreams and fears, and not just nameless avatars on a screen?

* Do I take moral responsibility for my words?

* Do I disagree with respect?

* Do I keep my feet on common ground while I speak?

* When someone has hurt me, do I address this hurt in a constructive way that does not transform them into an "enemy"?

WHEN LISTENING, ASK YOURSELF:

✳ Do I listen with my full attention?

✳ Do I listen with my mind, and with my heart?

✳ Do I listen mindfully, without immediately reacting to what is said?

✳ Do I listen without making another person's story all about myself?

✳ Do I listen with love and without judgment?

✳ Do I listen in a way that respects our differences?

✳ Do I listen for what unites us, rather than what divides?

✳ Do I listen to the words of my "enemies" and recognize that they hurt, too, just like me, and that they want to be happy, too, just like me?

Speaking and listening with love is a practical way to care for our interdependent life and for the people, creatures, and planet who share it. Remembering that words can hurt, and that they can also heal, and determining to speak words of care creates a culture of true democracy. Practicing democracy, we use our words as neither sticks nor stones. We use our words to affirm, to connect, and to heal. For democracy is not just the way to a better world. It also is that world—a world where we communicate wisely, a world where words are not weapons.

HATRED HAS NO PLACE *in* DEMOCRACY

Loving-kindness means
protecting the most vulnerable
members of your community.

The openness and welcoming spirit of democracy is not an invitation to suffer abuse. The communities we build must protect community members who are the most vulnerable to harm. Though mindfulness helps us to more skillfully relate to hate, no one need subject themselves to hateful words or physical menace in the name of being mindful.

The sad truth is not everyone recognizes that life is a miracle and that it is shared. Not everyone understands all being is inter-being. Some wrongly believe their independence is at war with interdependence. This is especially true of aspiring tyrants following bully rules. Even worse, many people, accustomed to thinking primarily about themselves and mistaking life for a zero-sum game, are hateful and abusive toward others.

How do healthy communities deal with hateful people? There is no easy answer to this question. A response that is too harsh and unforgiving forecloses the possibility for awakening, communication, and transcendence. A response that is too lenient and forgiving subjects the community to danger and potential dissolution. A middle way is required.

It would be easy to assume hateful people are too far gone to ever awaken to life as a shared miracle requiring shared attention and effort. Sometimes this is true; in many cases it is not. In my experience, most (though certainly not all) people who say stupid, hateful things do so out of habit—automatically, without thinking. Their hate often comes from an unexamined place of pain caused by the tremendous burden of living life under unjust rules, in the absence of true democracy and without the tender support of community. These people are mistaken, not evil. Care is called for when meeting such pain. Indeed, many people who are unwilling to participate in our shared life are not inherently vicious, they simply never learned how to relate to themselves or others in a healthy way.

A person acting unmindfully can be taught how to be mindful, a person behaving absent-mindedly can wake up to the miracle of life, a person who is out of control can be brought into greater balance, a person living heedlessly can be persuaded to see we are all in this together, a person speaking like a "knee-jerk" stuck in the grip of bad habits can learn to live more deliberately and less reactively. If we abandon the hope of being able to persuade the unmindful and to work with people who are sometimes "knee-jerks," we abandon the promise of democracy as a force of cultural change, too.

Anyone who insists on being hateful toward others behaves unmindfully and unethically. The hateful person who continues to behave cruelly and uses their words as weapons, even after others have repeatedly pointed out the hurt these choices cause, though, represents a danger to the Beloved Community and everyone who participates in it. I see no reason why a mindful community must bend over backward to include a person has revealed a full commitment to enemyship, and to pitting themselves and their own selfish interests against the well-being of others. Our communities might be forced to draw lines of who is welcome, and who is not. While no community should cheer such moments, we shouldn't shy away from them, either—healthy communities have an obligation to protect their members from hatred and abuse.

Hateful people today have successfully weaponized our culture's laudable urge to be more inclusive, diverse, equitable, and accessible in the communities we build. The hateful complain that shutting down their hate speech is a violation of guiding democratic ideals, including free speech. The hateful grumble that anyone who deprives them of the opportunity to spew verbal poison is a tyrant and a hypocrite (while at the same time trying to cancel the speech of others with whom they disagree). Having opened the door with talk of "educational freedom" and "intellectual openness" and being "fair and balanced," the hateful go to work trying to fracture and frustrate our communities' dedication to mindfulness, affirmation, and each other while openly abusing any people who look, think, believe, or speak differently from them.

Not all of us have the depth of practice and clarity of the Buddha; we do not all know when we can stand in the path of a killer and simply tell them that "we have stopped," as the Buddha said to Angulimala. So let's state this as clearly as possible: there is no need for a Beloved Community to include aspiring tyrants and belligerent bullies in the interest of being "fair and balanced." The right to free speech is not an excuse for people to speak, and act, time and time again, with hatred and violence. People who seek to destroy community cannot be allowed to do so just because they get offended when the community points out that they are trying to destroy it.

A person should be excluded: if they are unwilling to recognize life as a miracle and to acknowledge this miracle is shared, in spite of all the evidence that it is; if they are abusive and dismissive of their fellows, in word and deed; if they knowingly pursue their happiness in a way that causes others to suffer and denies to them the right to answer life's most fundamental questions in their own way.

Dealing with hatred is not an exact science. Your community might take a different path than mine, and that's to be expected, for life is lived locally, in particulars, not abstractions. Yet moments of exclusion must be moments of grave importance. This is no time for the community to act unmindfully. If we are forced to draw such lines, we must do so with care and attention, fully aware of all the unskillful ways society has excluded people in the past and determined not to repeat such injustice in the present.

IT IS A MARK OF WISDOM *to* PAUSE *and* ASK, "ARE YOU SURE?"

A mantra of mindful democracy is to
ask ourselves and others, "Are you sure?"
Remember this question before
moving from deliberation to action.

Mindful citizens do not act unless they are sure: sure they have correctly identified the roots of injustice, and sure their action will address injustice without bringing more suffering into the world. When I say "sure," I mean "sure enough." Sure enough we're comfortable with the path we've chosen. Sure enough we've deliberated about the options and this is the best course of action under the present circumstances. Sure enough the action we take will be consistent with our deepest held values. Sure enough we act out of lovingkindness, not anger or fear or hatred. Sure enough we're transforming the war, not intensifying it. Sure enough we stand on common ground.

Asking ourselves and others the question, "Are you sure?" is a mark of humility. Uncertainty is an existential condition. It can't be helped. The world is much bigger than we can perceive at any one moment. Simply put, we can't take it all in. Mindfulness practice reveals that every one of us is limited in how we view the world by our conditioning, and also by our bodies. When we deliberate together, we see the world more widely, from a higher vista, but the wisdom of communities, too, is limited. So we must be humble even while we stand tall on common ground.

Democracy requires us not to grasp so tightly to an idea that we're unwilling to listen to people who have different ideas; not so tightly that we're unwilling to change when change is warranted; not so tightly that we divide the world into friends who also believe what we do and enemies who don't; not so tightly that we cannot welcome others from different traditions into the community with a warm embrace; not so tightly that we go to war for our beliefs, forgetting the way of democracy. We must remember we can never be entirely sure, even as we check whether we are sure enough before we act.

There are ways to stand up for ourselves and for others that don't involve going to war.

To ask, "Are you sure?" slows us down even as the attention economy keeps trying to speed us up. This question builds in one more pause, one more chance to look deeply, before acting. It is a mindfulness bell. This question gives us a chance to be more considerate and thoughtful in word and deed so we do not add more suffering to the world as we attempt to relieve it.

Since the time of the Buddha, people committed to the path of mindfulness have agreed to live by a number of "precepts." These precepts, typically numbering five (the *pañcasīla*), provide a moral foundation for action.* They are not commandments from on high that must be obeyed unthinkingly. Rather, they are guidelines intended to prompt thoughtful consideration and practical exploration of what it means to live a shared, interdependent life.

In the Plum Village tradition, we call these precepts "The Five Mindfulness Trainings." Part of the first training is directly relevant the moment we choose to act: "Seeing that harmful actions arise from anger, fear, greed, and intolerance, which in turn come from dualistic and discriminative thinking, I will cultivate openness, nondiscrimination, and nonattachment to views in order to transform violence, fanaticism, and dogmatism in myself and in the world." To go to war for an idea—even if that idea is interbeing, or community, or democracy—is to forget that the world

---

* All five precepts are intended to cultivate a sense of interbeing: *ahimsa* (non-harming, non-wounding, non-killing, non-violence); *satya* (speaking truthfully); *asteya* (not stealing); *brahmacharya* (abstaining from sexual misconduct); and *sura* (clean eating and drinking, abstaining from intoxicants).

is both many and one, that every I is also a We, and that life is a shared miracle.

When we act, we must be sure we do not become fanatics or dogmatists who forget the strong foundations of our mindfulness practice. This is true for even the most devout Buddhists and the most devoted supporters of democracy. This does not mean we need to abandon our commitments. When it is time to stand up, we must stand tall! Yet we must also remember to ask ourselves and others:

"Are you sure?"

"Are you sure you are standing on common ground?"

"Are you sure you are acting with loving-kindness?"

"Are you sure you are not adding to the suffering of the world?"

"Are you sure you are practicing inclusion, and not exclusion?"

"Are you sure you are protecting the most vulnerable?"

"Are you sure you are getting to the roots of things?"

"Are you sure you are not acting in a way that creates a war?"

"Are you sure?"

MINDFUL ACTIONS AFFIRM *and* AWAKEN

There is no one right way to practice democracy. Democracy invites us to summon, and cultivate, the full range of human creativity. When we act, we do so in the spirit of affirmation, steadfast in our commitment to practice metta, to wake people up to injustice, and to persuade them not to participate in its continuation.

The flash of sunlight that inspires the lotus flower to begin its journey through the muddy waters is the light of collective awareness. When we act as a Beloved Community, the goal is to awaken our fellows, not to win a misbegotten political war. We act to bring injustice into the open, to expose it to sunlight, to make people aware of it and how it affects them, and to help them see it so clearly that they cannot deny it. Then we present a choice through our kind and loving presence: continue to silently support injustice (which hurts us all) or live to lessen the suffering of the world and enrich the shared miracle for us all.

It's not easy to open people's eyes, or to change people's minds, when they are determined to keep them closed, or when the inertia of habit is so strong that it rolls right over good intentions. The initial response to an argument for justice is usually, "No." If one's interlocutor is a bully, the response might be much more violent. So mindful citizens aim for more gradual change in others, even as we embrace the changes that happen in ourselves from our commitment to justice. As Dr. King wrote: "The nonviolent approach does not immediately change the heart of the oppressor. It first does something to the hearts and souls of those committed to it. It gives them new self-respect; it calls up resources of strength and courage they did not know they had. Finally, it reaches the opponent and so stirs his conscience that reconciliation becomes a reality."

Once the members of a Beloved Community determine to take a stand to address injustice and help those who are hurt by it, action can take many possible forms. The only limiting factors are our ethical commitments to each other and to the earth, which must be steadfast, and human creativity, which is boundless but which most of us are unskilled at exercising, especially together. Democracy invites us to be creative, to think outside the box, to break with convention and step outside our routines, habits, and assumptions of "this is how it must be done because that's how people have always done it." Democracy is serious; it is also playful. Keeping this sense of playfulness alive, even when we are addressing grave injustices, is essential.

Mindful citizens recognize that we cannot wait around for the universe to fix what is broken. Many people place their hope for righting injustice in a mysterious law of karma—an idea that, in the end, people cannot do wrong without suffering wrong, for the universe will set things right. Practicing mindful democracy, we understand that the word *karma* means *action*, not *acquiescence*. I share with you a poem I wrote that explores the dance of hope and action:

> **Karma Means Action**
> *Karma, are you there?*
> *We will wait expectantly*
> *But not in repose.*
>
> *When will we realize?*
> *The universe rarely bends*
> *It's us who make right.*

I know many people today want to do something to mend our fractured world; sometimes it can be hard to know where to start or what to do, when the problems seem so massive. In general, a good guideline for democratic action is to start local.

Learn about the challenges and injustices most immediate in your community and address them. Look for opportunities to build community, because the sorrows and injustices we face make no distinction between political affiliation: they affect us all. As you do, remain firm in your commitment to nonviolence, and continue to develop your personal and communal practice of mindfulness. Do not respond to violence with violence (physical or verbal)—this only invites more violence, and serves to legitimate the rule of bullies. Act as a beloved community, and keep each other safe.

The primary goal of democratic action is not to physically disrupt injustice, though if that can be done nonviolently, without enemyship, it is a worthy achievement. The goal of these actions is to draw disinterested and unmindful peoples' attention to injustice, to highlight how this unnecessary, human-caused suffering affects us all, and then to persuade our fellow beings not to participate in it. Having awakened ourselves to a more caring and loving way of life, the goal of democratic action is to awaken our fellows to this life as well. The way is affirmation, not destruction. Waging war cannot achieve this goal. It can only be achieved by awakening peoples' natural goodness rooted in the common ground we share: all of us suffer, and all of us want ourselves and the people we love to be safe, happy, and at peace.

Too often today political rhetoric is addressed to the aspects of people that are the weakest and ugliest, to their resentment, their hatred, their greed. Mindful citizens address the part of people that is capable of love, affection, and gratefulness, the part that reaches out for connection and cooperation, the expansive part that recognizes the beauty and wonder and mystery of this existence. Love, not hatred, is our common ground, and it is on this ground that we stand (and make our stand). Mindful citizens remember that we need not experience the world as a place of division and hatred, though we are habituated to do just this. Hatred is just as much a habit as love. Why should we judge the one inevitable, the other a luxury? Why make hatred our cultural baseline? We can stop and make a more mindful choice.

I have gathered a list of possible actions here, inspired by my two decades of scholarship on democracy and non-violence, as well as by the many students I've had the privilege of teaching and by courageous people all over the world who are walking the path of interdependence and doing the necessary work to keep the spirit of democracy, community, and mutual care alive (so much gratitude to you, wherever you are!).

Please do not take these suggestions for how you can practice true, mindful democracy as canonical or exclusive. They are not. I offer these suggestions in the spirit of heartfelt compassion, as a conversation starter and a potential source of inspiration for you and your community.

SPEAK POWERFUL, MINDFUL WORDS THAT ADDRESS OUR SHARED LIFE AND OUR OBLIGATIONS TO EACH OTHER:

* deliver public speeches;

* write letters in local and national media (traditional and social);

* create leaflets, pamphlets, placards, slogans, banners, posters, petitions, memes, floats, skywriting, earthwriting;

* give interviews;

* write books and articles;

* rewrite and reinvent important political documents (like the Declaration of Independence!) so they express true democracy;

* create and appear on podcasts;

* sign petitions;

* compose songs and plays and poetry;

* host a public debate about the issue at hand (as you do, practice the Five Agreements of Mindful Deliberation);

* write, direct, film a movie about interdependence that transcends political differences;

* compose meaningful social media posts;

* remind people of everything that unites us, and all the ways that we already support and protect each other;

* stage public forums where people who disagree can talk and explore the possibility that they are enemies only in their minds. . . .

PARTICIPATE IN MOVING SYMBOLIC PUBLIC ACTS THAT BRIGHTEN COLLECTIVE AWARENESS:

* create new holidays that commemorate important local historical moments when people cared for each other, in spite of their differences;

* celebrate community heroes who defend the spirit of democracy;

* put on a reading marathon focusing on important democratic texts or texts that that embody the qualities of mindful democracy;

* have an interdependence night at your local sporting event;

* stage a teach-in, a vigil, or a multifaith prayer and public worship service where people can learn from each other and bond in the practice of metta and compassion;

* organize mindfulness practice gatherings open to everyone;

* stage mock elections, awards, trials, or funerals that highlight injustice and those who perpetuate it;

* develop free public libraries where people can access censored or underappreciated works about interdependence;

* perform plays and skits, poetry readings, or communal concerts. . . .

PRACTICE PEACEFUL DEMONSTRATIONS IN THE SPIRIT OF NONVIOLENCE, ALL THE WHILE MEETING HATRED WITH LOVE, FOR EXAMPLE:

* parades

* marches

* picketing

* religious processions

* pilgrimages

* motorcades

* sit-ins

* community fasts

* collective civil disobedience

PARTICIPATE IN DEMOCRATIC GOVERNANCE:

* vote;

* civically educate yourself and your community concerning the ins and outs of local governance;

* learn how local rules, regulations, and laws are written (and how they can be changed);

* run for public office;

* work together with those in office and in the community to get laws that promote injustice and ignore the shared miracle of life changed;

* organize town halls;

* show up for public meetings to ask questions and hold representatives accountable;

* contact local officials to educate them about interdependence;

* know—and insist on—your constitutional rights;

* witness which officials stand for true democracy, and those who do not, and remember this on election day. . . .

AND, SOMETIMES, YOU NEED TO BE LIKE BARTLEBY—IN OTHER WORDS, SOMETIMES MINDFUL CITIZENS REFUSE; SOMETIMES THEY SAY "I WOULD PREFER NOT TO"* AND THEY:

* organize walk-outs, boycotts, strikes, and stay-at-home protests;

* refuse to shop or eat at businesses that support injustice (and promote businesses and organizations that support our shared life)—and make this refusal known with your powerful, compassionate words;

* choose not to consume content or to support an attention economy that undermines democracy and harms our interdependent life (and invite others to also participate in this choice);

* withhold assistance to agents of injustice;

* do not obey aspiring authoritarians who practice the rule of bullies in advance. . . .

When it comes to the challenge of caring for each other and for this life that we share, it's all hands on deck. Even small acts of kindness and compassion help to build a world that is freer, happier, and more at peace. If your community has decided to act, find something you're comfortable doing, stand on common ground, remember life is a shared miracle, and then act with loving-kindness!

---

* I call it this based on Herman Melville's 1853 short story "Bartleby, the Scrivener," in which the main character Bartleby repeatedly refuses to participate by saying "I would prefer not to."

═CONCLUSION═

If We See Things Clearly,
There Is Always Hope

The practice of mindfulness is not hard, but it can be hard to live a mindful life in a fractured, divided world that is out-of-balance and whose climate is growing warmer by the day. It takes courage to be present when the world prioritizes and rewards people for being unmindful. It takes a heart as big as a mountain to maintain one's commitment to living a happier life together when the world turns a blind eye toward injustice (or actively rewards it).

Democracy is hard. So many people aspire to be good citizens and start out strong, with the best intentions, only to throw their hands up and say "enough!" when confronted by a recalcitrant world. Can you see these moments of frustration as a crossroads? If you find yourself discouraged and downhearted, and are tempted to cede your agency and freedom to an unjust status quo, please know you have the power to handle these feelings without giving up. If burnout comes, you are ready: embody what you've learned from your practice of mindfulness; attend to your material needs; return to your Beloved Community for support and refuge; focus on the creative arts to recharge your batteries; do something that nourishes your spirit and connects you to the earth.

In moments of challenge and despair, ask yourself what gives you hope. Ask others this question, too. Let it become a conversation in your community. Write the answers down. Return to them when strength feels out of reach. Here, you might look to history—the history of the world, and your own history. Each of us has moments in our biography where we faced a challenge and came out stronger. History proves the power of mindfulness and democracy. There have been moments when mindful citizens have worked together to address injustice and make the world both happier and less painful. Search these moments out. Study them. Learn from them. Let them become another source of hope in the present moment.

If you hear the voices of desperation, depression, and nihilism arising in your mind, remember to tap into the deep wellsprings of hope.

For hope is a practice. It is, like gratitude and love, something that we nourish.

This hope is not groundless. It is rooted in the change we experience in our own practice, and in the connections we forge when we build community to practice, deliberate, and act together. The conditions for hope are already here. Slow down and look deeply, and you will see them.

I leave you with a poem I wrote during the darkest days of winter in the Allegheny Mountains of central Pennsylvania, when the sun did not show itself for two weeks and an icy drizzle made it dangerous to be outside. At precisely the moment my spirits needed a lift, I looked out the window into our backyard and saw a drop of water fall to the ground from a branch of one of the many Japanese maple trees I planted that one day might become bonsai. At that moment I stopped dreaming of spring and felt the warmth that was already here, the warmth of mindful, loving presence, the warmth that comes from awakening to interdependence.

Hope
Snow melts from a tree branch
Someday soon it will be a cloud
And rain will fall on new leaves

There is spring in winter,
And winter in spring
Take heart

Having together declared our interdependence, and having pledged to care for each other and for the life we share, this is where we part for now, dear friends. I leave you in the fortuitous space between now and next, between today and tomorrow, between a present so real you can reach out and touch it and a future that is never guaranteed but that responds to loving, mindful action. The space of freedom. The space of responsibility. The space of choice. The space of community. The space of mindfulness: which, when life is rightly viewed as a shared project that begins from common ground, is also the space of democracy.

My friends,

May your life be a gentle unfolding into goodness and gladness and gratefulness.

May the bumpy road lead you to greater freedom, connection, and peace.

May your words be bridges, not battlegrounds.

May your breath remind you of the miracle it is to be alive in this body, in this moment, among these people.

May your hands be instruments of care, your eyes tuned to wonder, your presence a balm to the weary.

May you find the courage to speak when silence feeds injustice,

And the humility to listen when wisdom is not your own.

May you remember, always, that you are not alone (because you are not alone)—

That this life is shared,

That this work is shared,

And that together, we are already the beginning of the world we long for.

Go softly. Go bravely. Go together.

TEAR HERE

═NOTES═

INTRODUCTION: TRUE DEMOCRACY SLUMBERS IF WE DO. LET US BE AWAKE!

1 Walt Whitman, *Democratic Vistas* (1871), in *Complete Poetry and Collected Prose*, ed. Justin Kaplan (Library of America, 1982), 960. (Page 1.)

2 For helpful scholarly background on the Declaration of Independence, see Pauline Maier, *American Scripture: Making the Declaration of Independence* (Knopf, 1998), and Danielle Allen, *Our Declaration: A Reading of the Declaration of Independence in Defense of Equality* (Norton, 2014). (Page 2.)

3 David Armitage, *The Declaration of Independence: A Global History* (Harvard University Press, 2007). The Declaration also inspired Americans—farmers, labor activists, abolitionists, suffragettes, socialists, civil rights activists—to craft alternative, more radical documents: see Philip S. Foner, ed., *We, the Other People: Alternative Declarations of Independence by Labor Groups, Farmers, Women's Rights Advocates, Socialists, and Blacks 1829–1975* (University of Illinois Press, 1976). (Page 3.)

4 Through careful archival research, Jay Fliegelman demonstrates that the Declaration of Independence was intended to be read aloud and performed publicly in *Declaring Independence: Jefferson, Natural Language, and the Culture of Performance* (Stanford University Press, 1993). (Page 3.)

5 I describe how the rhetoric of enemyship works in my first two books: Jeremy Engels, *Enemyship: Democracy and Counter-Revolution in the Early Republic* (Michigan State University Press, 2010), and Jeremy Engels, *The Politics of Resentment: A Genealogy* (Penn State University Press, 2015). (Page 3.)

6 My understanding of democracy is inspired by the pragmatist philosophy of John Dewey and Cornel West, which has deep roots in the American experience; by the compassionate, expansive, sky-blue poetry of Walt Whitman; by the Engaged Buddhism of Thich Nhat Hanh and the Plum Village tradition; by the nonviolent activism of Gandhi, Martin Luther King, Jr, and James Lawson; and by the brilliant work of many philosophers (including many

of my wonderful colleagues at Penn State University) in the field of "care ethics." For a powerful statement of democracy's true potential, see Cornel West, *Democracy Matters* (Penguin, 2005); on Engaged Buddhism, see Thich Nhat Hanh, *Good Citizens: Creating Enlightened Society* (Parallax Press, 2012). (Page 5.)

7 Nhat Hanh, *Good Citizens*, 2. (Page 7.)

8 Thomas Merton, Address to International Summit of Monks, Calcutta, India (October 19–27, 1968), in *The Asian Journals of Thomas Merton* (New Directions, 1975), 51. (Page 7.)

9 Bhagavad Gita, 11.1, 7.27 (we are deluded, Krishna teaches here, "by duality delusion" (*dvandvamohena*)). On the yogic rhetorics of oneness, see Jeremy David Engels, *The Ethics of Oneness: Emerson, Whitman, and the Bhagavad Gita* (University of Chicago Press, 2021). (Page 7.)

10 Here, see Jeremy David Engels, *Living Namaste: A Practical Guide to Mindfulness, Yoga, and Building Community* (Inner Traditions, 2026). (Page 7.)

11 Robin Wall Kimmerer, *Braiding Sweetgrass: Indigenous Wisdom, Scientific Knowledge, and the Teachings of Plants* (Milkweed, 2013), 15. (Page 7.)

12 Einstein quoted in Walter Sullivan, "The Einstein Papers. A Man of Many Parts," *New York Times*, March 29, 1972. For a more recent argument that physics leads to a similar insight, see Heinrich Pas, *The One: How an Ancient Idea Holds the Future of Physics* (Basic Books, 2023). (Page 7.)

13 In traditional meditation texts including the Satipatthana Sutta, the "Sutra on Mindfulness," mindfulness involves two practices: calming the mind (*shamatha*) and looking deeply (*vipassana*). Once the mind becomes calm (*shamatha*), it is possible to realize *vipassana*, insight. In the ancient Pali language, *vi-* means "clear," and *passana* means "perceiving," so *vipassana* is a practice of perceiving life clearly. And when you see things clearly, insight becomes possible. In this way, *mindfulness reveals the reality of interbeing—or what I call in this book interdependence.* (Page 8.)

14 Thich Nhat Hanh, *The Diamond That Cuts through Illusion: Commentaries on the Prajnaparamita Diamond Sutra* (Parallax Press, 2010), 44. (Page 9.)

INSIGHT 1: LIFE IS A MIRACLE

15 Thich Nhat Hanh, *The Miracle of Mindfulness: An Introduction to the Practice of Mindfulness* (1975; Beacon Press, 1987), 12. (Page 20.)

INSIGHT 2: DEMOCRACY IS HOW WE CARE

16 You might say, then, that to practice democracy is to practice "justice," which mindfulness teacher and scholar Rhonda Magee defines as the determination to put "love in action for the alleviation of suffering." Rhonda V. Magee, *The Inner Work of Racial Justice: Healing Ourselves and Our Communities through Mindfulness* (Tarcher Perigee, 2019), 6. (Page 26.)

INSIGHT 3: IN A DISTRACTED WORLD, BEING PRESENT IS REVOLUTIONARY

17 Mark Williams and Danny Penman , *Mindfulness: An 8-Week Plan for Finding Peace in a Frantic World* (Rodale: 2012); Thich Nhat Hanh, *The Miracle of Mindfulness* (Beacon Press, 1999); Tara Brach, *Radical Compassion: Learning to Love Yourself and Your World with the Practice of RAIN* (Penguin, 2020); Rhonda Magee, "The S.T.O.P. Practice: Creating Space Around Automatic Reactions," *Mindful.org*, March 23, 2020. (Page 28.)

18 Daniel Goleman and Richard J. Davidson, *Altered Traits: Science Reveals How Meditation Changes Your Mind, Brain, and Body* (Penguin, 2018). (Page 29.)

19 David Gelles, *Mindful Work: How Meditation Is Changing Business from the Inside Out* (HMH, 2015). (Page 29.)

20 Ronald E. Purser, *McMindfulness: How Mindfulness Became the New Capitalist Spirituality* (Repeater, 2019); *What's Wrong with Mindfulness (and What Isn't)*, ed. Barry Magid and Robert Rosenbaum (Wisdom, 2016). (Page 29.)

21 Stephen Batchelor, *Buddhism Without Beliefs: A Contemporary Guide to Awakening* (Riverhead Books, 1997), 7–18. (Page 29.)

22 For a brilliant history of Buddhism, see Donald S. Lopez, Jr., *Buddhism: A Journey Through History* (Yale University Press, 2024). (Page 30.)

23 For Buddhists, there is a path that leads us where we want to go. It is a well-trod path that many others before us have walked, a path with plenty of signage, a path that is best walked hand-in-hand and arm-in-arm with others in community. This noble path is a path of spiritual exercise, and it includes eight practices: right view, right thinking, right speech, right action, right diligence, right concentration, right mindfulness, and right livelihood. Although it is traditionally placed seventh on the agenda, Thich Nhat Hanh suggests that mindfulness could be placed first, since the noble path asks us to take every step in mindfulness (*Good Citizens*, 71). Buddhists consider mindfulness as one part of a more comprehensive practice that touches on all aspects

of our lives — how we think, the words we say, what we eat, the kinds of jobs we take, how we meditate, the friends we keep, how we love, how we spend our time. The goal of this practice is to alleviate suffering, so that we can fully experience and enjoy the shared miracle of life. (Page 30.)

24   On Engaged Buddhism, see Thich Nhat Hanh, *Good Citizens: Creating Enlightened Society* (Parallax Press, 2012). (Page 31.)

INSIGHT 5: THERE IS NO LOTUS WITHOUT MUD

25   See the Bhaddekaratta Sutta, translated as "Discourse on Knowing the Better Way to Live Alone" in Thich Nhat Hanh, *Chanting from the Heart: Buddhist Ceremonies and Daily Practices* (Parallax Press, 2007), 282–284. (Page 38.)

INSIGHT 8: WHAT WE PAY ATTENTION TO MATTERS

26   Jenny Odell, *How to Do Nothing: Resisting the Attention Economy* (Melville House, 2020). (Page 50.)

27   Buddhist speak of "four nutriments" that give us fuel—edible food, sense impressions, intentions, and consciousness. Thich Nhat Hanh, *The Heart of the Buddha's Teaching: Transforming Suffering into Peace, Joy, and Liberation* (Broadway Books, 1998), 31–38. With great skill, the Plum Village dharma teacher Kaira Jewel Lingo uses the metaphor of a house to describe the fourth nutriment, consciousness—see Kaira Jewel Lingo, *We Were Made for These Times: 10 Lessons for Moving Through Change, Loss, and Disruption* (Parallax Press, 2021), 52. (Page 52.)

INSIGHT 9: THE ON-RAMP IS WHEREVER YOU ARE NOW

28   Thich Nhat Hanh, *Old Path White Clouds: Walking in the Footsteps of the Buddha* (Parallax Press, 1991), 152. (Page 59.)

INSIGHT 10: GRATITUDE IS THE FOUNDATIONAL DEMOCRATIC EMOTION

29   I take up the questions of how to break bread, how to knock down philosophical, political, and spiritual walls, and how to build relationships across differences and divisions, in my forthcoming book: Jeremy David Engels, *Living Namaste: A Practical Guide to Mindfulness, Yoga, and Building Community* (Inner Traditions, 2026). It all starts with a mindful "hello."(Page 62.)

30   Jeremy David Engels, *The Art of Gratitude* (SUNY Press, 2018). (Page 63.)

INSIGHT 11: DEMOCRACY REQUIRES STRONG AND OPEN HEARTS

31 Sharon Salzburg, *Lovingkindness: The Revolutionary Art of Happiness* (Shambhala, 2002), 24–25. (Page 69.)

32 Jeremy Engels, *The Art of Gratitude* (State University of New York Press, 2018). (Page 69.)

33 In the fifth century CE, a Sri Lankan Buddhist monk named Buddhaghosa composed an important meditation text called the *Visuddhimagga*, or "The Path of Purification." In this text Buddhaghosa provides instructions for how to practice loving-kindness meditation, and contemporary teachers adapt and modify these instructions to best meet the needs of their communities. (Page 69.)

34 The Buddha used the Pali term *sabbattataya*, "being at one with everything," to describe the effect of practicing loving-kindness. Thich Nhat Hanh, *Teachings on Love*, 49, quoting Majjhima Nikaya, Sutta 99. (Page 70.)

INSIGHT 12: DEMOCRACY STARTS WHEN WE STOP LIVING A LIE

35 Systems of class and caste are based on a misunderstanding of the human condition: for no one is inherently better than anyone else. Equality is the human condition. Indeed, as anthropologist David Graeber and archeologist David Wengrow argue in their important book *The Dawn of Everything: A New History of Humanity* (Farrar, Straus, and Giroux, 2021), inequality is not inevitable as societies grow and develop (though many popular myths from the European Enlightenment insist that it is). For a brilliant discussion of how caste societies function, see Isabel Wilkerson, *Caste: The Origins of Our Discontents* (Random House, 2020); for a description of how mindfulness practice can help to transform the injustice of racial caste systems, see Larry Ward, *America's Racial Karma: An Invitation to Heal* (Parallax Press, 2020), and Rhonda Magee, *The Inner Work of Racial Justice* (Tarcher, 2021). (Page 74.)

INSIGHT 13: IT IS IN BELOVED COMMUNITIES THAT WE LEARN TO PRACTICE DEMOCRACY

36 For a helpful history of the Beloved Community, see Marc Andrus, *Brothers in the Beloved Community: The Friendship of Thich Nhat Hanh and Martin Luther King, Jr.* (Parallax Press, 2021). (Page 76.)

37 Beloved Community is an aspiration that predates both King and Nhat Hanh and emerges from the long and proud tradition of peace and civil rights activism in the United States during the twentieth- and twenty-first centuries. The Harvard philosopher Josiah Royce first described Beloved Communities around the time of World War I, imagining communities built on love and compassion, rather than resentment and division. The union organizer and minister A. J. Muste, a founder of the American branch of the Fellowship of Reconciliation and later its president, worked to transform Royce's philosophical vision into reality. The Black theologian and civil rights activist Howard Thurman continued the lineage with his work and writings, revealing how Beloved Community could be a path to worldly justice. Muste and Thurman introduced the aspiration for Beloved Community to a young preacher named Martin Luther King, Jr., who made it central to his rhetoric and activism during the Civil Rights Movement. King, in turn, welcomed Nhat Hanh into this project, just as Thầy has welcomed me and many others. (Page 76.)

39 Martin Luther King Jr., "Loving Your Enemies," in *Strength to Love* (1963; Beacon Press, 2019), 53. (Page 77.)

INSIGHT 15: EVERY I IS ALSO A WE

40 American Academy of Achievement interview with Wynton Marsalis, January 8, 1991, *https://wyntonmarsalis.org/news/entry/academy-of-achievement -interview-with-wynton-marsalis*. (Page 84.)

41 John Dewey, *The Public and Its Problems* (1927; Swallow Press, 1954), 184. (Page 84.)

42 I describe the power of Whitman's democratic poetry in more detail in my book Jeremy David Engels, *The Ethics of Oneness: Emerson, Whitman, and the Bhagavad Gita* (University of Chicago Press, 2021). (Page 85.)

43 Walt Whitman, "Song of Myself." (Page 85.)

44 Walt Whitman, "Song of the Open Road." (Page 85.)

INSIGHT 16: WE ARE ONE, AND WE ARE MANY

45 I make a detailed argument for this ethical position in my book Jeremy David Engels, *The Ethics of Oneness: Emerson, Whitman, and the Bhagavad Gita* (University of Chicago Press, 2021). (Page 88.)

INSIGHT 17: ENEMYSHIP WRECKS DEMOCRACY BY TRANSFORMING IT INTO WAR

46 A word about "rhetoric," from a professor of this misunderstood art. Most people tend to think "rhetoric" means either fluff or deception (or worse).

But really, rhetoric is the skillful use of language and other symbols to get things done. Anytime we build a relationship or a community or a team, anytime we pump up the troops for war or persuade them to put down their arms for peace, anytime we rally people for change, we use rhetoric. Rhetoric is a basic building block of social life. It is folk wisdom in our culture to say *if you can dream it, you can do it,* but that's not quite true—you also have to be able to *speak it.* It is here that so many people fail, for they have not yet learned to harness the power of rhetoric. Like any art, rhetoric can be used for good or ill. When used for good, rhetoric allows us to live together in harmony and to work together democratically. (Page 92.)

47 Jeremy Engels, *Enemyship: Democracy and Counter-Revolution in the Early Republic* (Michigan State University Press, 2010). (Page 92.)

INSIGHT 18: NO PERSON IS "EVIL," ONLY "MISTAKEN"
48 Nhat Hanh, *Old Path White Clouds*, 351–358. (Page 97.)

INSIGHT 19: THERE IS NO WAY TO DEMOCRACY, DEMOCRACY IS THE WAY
49 Ramin Jahanbegloo, *The Gandhian Moment* (Harvard University Press, 2013), 42. (Page 104.)

INSIGHT 20: MINDFUL CITIZENS CARE: WE DO NOT ACQUIESCE TO INJUSTICE OR BOW TO THE STATUS QUO
50 Henry David Thoreau, "Civil Disobedience."(Page 108.)

51 On the Order of Interbeing, see Thich Nhat Hanh, *Interbeing: The 14 Mindfulness Trainings of Engaged Buddhism*, 4th Edition (Parallax Press, 2020). (Page 109.)

52 Thich Nhat Hanh to Martin Luther King, Jr., June 1, 1965, quoted in Andrus, *Brothers in the Beloved Community*, 20. (Page 109.)

53 For this powerful and moving story, see Sister Chan Khong, *Learning True Love: Practicing Buddhism in a Time of War* (Parallax Press, 1993). (Page 109.)

54 Thich Nhat Hanh, *Good Citizens*, 3. For an engaging look at Zen reformers, see Perle Besserman and Manfred B. Steiger, *Zen Radicals, Rebels, and Reformers* (Wisdom Press, 2011). Jon Kabat-Zinn, the founder of the Mindfulness Based Stress Reduction program and one of the people most responsible for mindfulness's global popularity, makes a similar point. He

cautions that we must be "careful" that we do not mistake mindful acceptance of the present moment with the acceptance of injustice: "Acceptance doesn't, by any stretch of the imagination, mean passive resignation. Quite the opposite. It takes a huge amount of fortitude and motivation to accept what is—especially when you don't like it—and then work wisely and effectively as best you possibly can with the circumstances you find yourself in and with the resources at your disposal, both inner and outer, to mitigate, heal, redirect, and change what can be changed." Or, in the words of Jack Kornfield, one of the mindfulness teachers I've had the privilege to study with, "Acceptance is not passivity. It is a courageous step in the process of transformation." Jon Kabat-Zinn, *Coming to Our Senses: Healing Ourselves and the World Through Mindfulness* (Hyperion, 2005), 407; Jack Kornfield, *The Wise Heart: A Guide to the Universal Teachings of Buddhist Psychology* (Bantam, 2009), 102. (Page 110.)

INSIGHT 21: DEMOCRACY IS ABOUT WINNING HEARTS, NOT WARS

55 Erica Chenoweth and Maria Stephan, *Why Civil Resistance Works: The Strategic Logic of Nonviolent Conflict* (Columbia University Press, 2012); Erica Chenoweth, *Civil Resistance: What Everyone Needs to Know* (Oxford University Press, 2021). (Page 113.)

56 Sudarshan Kapur, *Raising Up a Prophet: The African-American Encounter with Gandhi* (Beacon Press, 1992), and Nico Slate, *Colored Cosmopolitanism: The Shared Struggle for Freedom in the United States and India* (Harvard University Press, 2012). (Page 113.)

57 Martin Luther King, Jr., "Pilgrimage to Nonviolence," in *A Testament of Hope: The Essential Writings of Martin Luther King, Jr.*, ed. James M. Washington (HarperOne, 1986), 39. (Page 114.)

58 Martin Luther King, Jr., *Stride Toward Freedom* (1958), in *A Testament of Hope*, 447. (Page 114.)

59 Richard Gregg, *The Power of Non-Violence* (J. B. Lippincott, 1934), 41–54. (Page 115.)

INSIGHT 22: DELIBERATION IS THE CORNERSTONE OF DEMOCRACY

60 Every semester, my academic home, the Department of Communication Arts and Sciences at Penn State University, teaches students how to

deliberate in a number of classes, including a required course called "Rhetoric and Civic Life." This course is organized around a set of deliberative guidelines that most instructors share with their students. These guidelines are so deeply ingrained in my departmental culture that no one knows who created them anymore. Some of the amazing people I know were involved in generating these guidelines include Lori Bedell, Ben Henderson, Jessica O'Hara, David Hutchinson, Sara Drury, Rosa Eberly, and John Gastil. These guidelines were the original inspiration for the deliberative agreements I wrote. Unlike many deliberation scholars, I think of them not as rules an authority figure imposes on the proceedings but as agreements participants voluntarily accede to so our deliberations are as wise and skillful as possible or, to put it another way, mindful. My version of these guidelines is deeply influenced by my other academic home at Penn State, the Rock Ethics Institute, which emphasizes the importance of considering multiple (and not just human) stakeholders whenever we make decisions. (Page 119.)

INSIGHT 24: THE TRUE POWER OF WORDS IS MENDING

61 In our Beloved Communities, it is essential that we practice loving speech and mindful listening. For helpful guides to these practices, see Thich Nhat Hanh, *The Art of Communicating* (HarperOne, 2013), and Sister Chan Khong, *Beginning Anew: Four Steps to Restoring Communication* (Parallax Press, 2014). (Page 124.)

INSIGHT 25: HATRED HAS NO PLACE IN DEMOCRACY

62 Here, see Bradford Vivian, *Campus Misinformation: The Real Threat to Free Speech in American Higher Education* (Oxford University Press, 2022). (Page 136.)

INSIGHT 26: IT IS A MARK OF WISDOM TO PAUSE AND ASK, "ARE YOU SURE?"

63 Thich Nhat Hanh, *Interbeing*, 146. (Page 141.)

INSIGHT 27: MINDFUL ACTIONS AFFIRM AND AWAKEN

64 King, "Pilgrimage to Nonviolence," 39. (Page 144.)

65 For an exploration of the dynamics of karma and acquiescence in the context of democracy, see Engels, *The Ethics of Oneness*, 141–195. (Page 145.)

66 My suggestions are inspired by the brilliant work of my fellow nonviolence
    scholars, including the University of Massachusetts political scientist Gene
    Sharp, who catalogued 198 methods of creative, nonviolent, democratic
    action in his powerful 1973 book *The Politics of Nonviolent Action*. One of the
    most influential scholars of nonviolence in the twentieth century, Sharp was
    nominated for the Nobel Peace Prize several times, and in 2008 he received
    the International Courage of Conscience Award from the Peace Abbey
    Foundation. Sharp studied the history of nonviolence to create his list, which
    divided action into five categories: "nonviolent protest and persuasion";
    "social noncooperation"; "economic noncooperation: boycotts"; "economic
    noncooperation: strikes"; and "political noncooperation." Gene Sharp, *The
    Politics of Nonviolent Action*, Part Two: *The Methods of Nonviolent Action*
    (Beacon, 1973). A big shout-out to my dear friend, the brilliant scholar
    Amentahru Wahlrab, who is my frequent conversation partner about all
    questions related to the powers and possibilities of nonviolence. (Page 145.)

CONCLUSION: IF WE SEE THINGS CLEARLY, THERE IS ALWAYS HOPE

67 For more helpful practices for managing burnout, see Brother Phap Huu
    and Jo Confino, *Being with Busyness: Zen Ways to Transform Overwhelm and
    Burnout* (Parallax Press, 2024). (Page 153.)

68 The writer and activist Rebecca Solnit has written several books about the
    historical basis for hope: in particular, *Hope in the Dark* (Nation Books,
    2004) and *A Paradise Built in Hell: The Extraordinary Communities That
    Arise in Disaster* (Viking: 2009). (Page 154.)

=ACKNOWLEDGMENTS=

In the United States, where I was born and live, we are raised from a young age to be rugged individuals. We are taught that each of us is solely and personally responsible for our successes and failures, and that if you want to get ahead in life, you had better cowboy up. A character in Kurt Vonnegut's comic novel *Slapstick* explains the American ethos in the following terms: "In case nobody has told you . . . this is the United States of America, where nobody has a right to rely on anybody else—where everybody learns to make his or her own way." This philosophy—of pulling yourself up by your bootstraps, of paddling your own canoe, of going it alone—is supposed to inspire us to work hard so we get ahead and find the happiness we pursue with such vigor, but in reality, it makes for a lonely and unnecessarily hard life. In fact, it places much more weight on our individual backs than we need to bear.

Practicing mindfulness, I've come to understand just how wrongheaded and misguided rugged (ragged?) individualism really is. We do not live in spite of others or in opposition to them; we live with them and because of them. None of us is alone, not really. None of us has to walk life's path in isolation, and even when we think we are walking alone we are not (ask yourself: Who made your shoes? Who carved the trail? Who created the map? Who invented the words on the map and the trail markers?). We are all a part of something much bigger than ourselves, a beloved community that spans centuries and continents, a community that, when it gets its act together, will change the world.

As my mindfulness practice has deepened, so too has my experience of gratitude. Contemplating all the people, and all the beings, who support and sustain me, I find myself overcome by my love of my comrades, and by such gladness that I and they exist. To everyone, and everything, that made this book possible, I extend a big Walt Whitman-sized hug of multitudes and my deepest, most profound thanksgiving.

Thanks to my dearest love, Anna Sunderland Engels, my best friend, my wife, my everything, my other half, my brilliant, beautiful, generous, kind-hearted, witty, world-traveling, photo-snapping, fashion-designing, small business–running partner. To me, Anna is the sun. I love you, and I am blessed to spend my days by your side. Anna read every word of this book multiple times, and it is so much better for it (add "editor" to her long list of talents!). Thanks to my family and to Anna's family, for their kindness, generosity, warmth, and smiles. Thanks to my oldest friend, Andy Shaner, for always being there for me. Thanks to all my friends in State College who supported me as I wrote this book. Thanks to my buddies Kevin Hulburt and Peter Buck for the hikes and camaraderie. Thanks to my amazing neighbors for their friendship and all the laughs. Thanks to the brilliant people at Yoga Lab, my community, my sangha. Anna and I started this studio in 2016 with friends, and one in particular deserves a special shout-out—Kristen Boccumini, thanks for being a dear friend, and for all the feedback and encouragement you offered me while I was writing this book! And thanks to my dear friend Lara Heimann for teaching me a better way to practice, and teach, yoga.

ACKNOWLEDGMENTS

I first took up meditation in high school, though it was many years after that before I knew what I was doing. In many ways, this book is a homecoming of sorts for me. I wrote an essay on nonviolence in high school that drew on American Transcendentalism and Zen Buddhism that won a gold medal at National History Day under the guidance and direction of the poet Andrew Davis, my all-time favorite teacher and my greatest inspiration. Every time that I enter the classroom, I think to myself, if I can only be half as good a teacher as Andrew, I will have done my job today! As an undergraduate at the University of Kansas, I was fortunate to be mentored by the brilliant communication scholar Gregory Shepherd, and it was in Greg's classes that I first encountered the democratic theory that still, to this day, inspires me to think of better ways to be in the world. To Andrew and Kay Davis of Wichita, and to Greg Shepherd, you are my academic family, and I love you.

Thank you to the members of the global Plum Village community for inspiring me to write this book—in particular, thanks go to my friend Shantum Seth, dharma teacher and leader of pilgrimages. In December 2023, I traveled to Vietnam with Shantum's nonprofit Buddhapath to visit Thich Nhat Hanh's birthplace and root temple. On the journey out of Huế, we stopped at the spot where Thầy was cremated, spending the morning in meditation and conversation. Roasting under the hot morning sun, I became aware of a butterfly flitting from flower to flower, and shoulder to shoulder. It was so beautiful! Later, on the bus I wrote a poem ("A Lovely Morning at the Crematorium"); when I got back to Pennsylvania, I submitted it for publication in *The Mindfulness Bell*. And then I completely forgot about it. Almost a year later, the poetry editor, Heather Weightman, wrote to let

me know the poem was being published! And the very next day, an editor at Parallax Press, Miranda Perrone, contacted me—she read my poem, loved it, and wanted to talk about working on a book together. This book was born out of that conversation. A big thank you to Miranda—it has been a joy working with you, and I feel such appreciation for the loving attention you paid to this book from idea to finished manuscript. And many lotus flowers to everyone at Parallax. It has been a lot of fun working with you on this project. Throughout the process, my literary agent, Anne Marie O'Farrell, has stood by my side, offering wise advice and counsel. Thank you for believing in me, and for your encouragement and support.

I am blessed to work for Penn State University, nestled in the Allegheny Mountains of central Pennsylvania in a place we lovingly call Happy Valley. I've been exploring the relationship between mindfulness and democracy for many years now, and my research, and teaching, has been supported by my academic home, The Department of Communication Arts and Sciences, and by three interdisciplinary research centers at Penn State: the Rock Ethics Institute, the Center for Democratic Deliberation, and the Humanities Institute. The tireless support of my department heads and dear friends Denise Solomon and Kirt Wilson gave me the courage to walk this path. Gratitude to my colleagues at Penn State and beyond for your kindness. Thanks to Ira Allen, Nathan Crick, and Scott Stroud, my favorite interlocutors. Thanks to Amentahru Wahlrab, for reading my chapters on nonviolence and for being a dear friend. Thanks to Jennie Rothenberg Gritz for many enlightening conversations about meditation. Thanks to my friends in the Center for Research in Modernity in Transition, including Ben Schewel and Shahrzad Sabet, for the encouragement and stimulating conversation. And a big thank you to all my students, without whom this book would not exist. In particular, I'd like to thank two PhD students I'm privileged to work with—Lynsey Medd and Isaac Richards—who both read parts of the book and provided valuable feedback. Keep an eye out for these two; they are future thought leaders.

To everyone mentioned here, to everyone whom I forgot to mention, to everyone who supports me, to everyone who contributes to the commonweal and does what they are able to nurture the common ground on which we stand, I extend my love, my kindness, and my gratitude. I pledge to work with you and alongside you to make sure that everyone has the support they need to live, because, ultimately, we are all in this together.

=ABOUT THE AUTHOR=

 JEREMY DAVID ENGELS, PhD, is Liberal Arts Professor of Communication and Ethics at Pennsylvania State University. He is an award-winning scholar who has published numerous books and articles about democracy, community building, deliberation, and peace, including *The Ethics of Oneness*, *The Art of Gratitude*, and *Living Namaste*. He is also a long-time teacher of mindfulness, meditation, and yoga, having studied in both India and the United States. Since undertaking a pilgrimage to walk in the footsteps of the Buddha in India and Nepal in 2018, he has been a student of Thích Nhất Hạnh. A beloved teacher, he is affectionately known by his students as the "bed-headed professor" and "the yoga prof," and his classes have been described as "*Mister Rogers' Neighborhood* meets Walt Whitman, *Zen and the Art of Motorcycle Maintenance*, and *The Good Place*."

Engels lives in State College, Pennsylvania, where he and his wife, Anna Sunderland Engels, run a community yoga and meditation studio called Yoga Lab. He is an experienced *asana* teacher whose yoga teaching integrates a deep understanding of functional movement with mindfulness. Though Yoga Lab, he has been training yoga and meditation teachers for more than a decade. Jeremy enjoys spending his free time gardening, writing poetry, practicing yoga, hiking, cooking, and tending to his bonsai trees. Jeremy joyfully joins the Plum Village Beloved Community in practicing mindfulness as "the practice of peace."

www.jeremydavidengels.com

Monastics and visitors practice the art of mindful living in the tradition of Thich Nhat Hanh at our mindfulness practice centers around the world. To reach any of these communities, or for information about how individuals, couples, and families can join in a retreat, please contact:

PLUM VILLAGE
24240 Thénac, France
plumvillage.org

LA MAISON DE L'INSPIR
77510 Villeneuve-sur-Bellot, France
maisondelinspir.org

HEALING SPRING MONASTERY
77510 Verdelot, France
healingspringmonastery.org

MAGNOLIA GROVE MONASTERY
Batesville, MS 38606, USA
magnoliagrovemonastery.org

BLUE CLIFF MONASTERY
Pine Bush, NY 12566, USA
bluecliffmonastery.org

DEER PARK MONASTERY
Escondido, CA 92026, USA
deerparkmonastery.org

EUROPEAN INSTITUTE OF APPLIED BUDDHISM
D-51545 Waldbröl, Germany
eiab.eu

THAILAND PLUM VILLAGE
*Nakhon Ratchasima
30130 Thailand*
thaiplumvillage.org

ASIAN INSTITUTE OF APPLIED BUDDHISM
Lantau Island, Hong Kong
pvfhk.org

STREAM ENTERING MONASTERY
Porcupine Ridge, Victoria 3461 Australia
nhapluu.org

MOUNTAIN SPRING MONASTERY
Bilpin, NSW 2758, Australia
mountainspringmonastery.org

For more information visit: *plumvillage.org*
To find an online sangha visit: *plumline.org*
For more resources, try the Plum Village app: *plumvillage.app*
Social media: *@thichnhathanh @plumvillagefrance*

PARALLAX PRESS, a nonprofit publisher founded by Zen Master Thich Nhat Hanh, publishes books and media on the art of mindful living and Engaged Buddhism. We are committed to offering teachings that help transform suffering and injustice. Our aspiration is to contribute to collective insight and awakening, bringing about a more joyful, healthy, and compassionate society.

View our entire library at parallax.org.

THE MINDFULNESS BELL is a journal of the art of mindful living in the Plum Village tradition of Thich Nhat Hanh. To subscribe or to see the worldwide directory of Sanghas (local mindfulness groups), visit mindfulnessbell.org.